JOURNEY WITH ME

Journey With Me

Diane M. McDonald

iUniverse, Inc.
New York Lincoln Shanghai

Journey With Me

iUniverse books may be ordered through booksellers or by contacting:

iUniverse
2021 Pine Lake Road, Suite 100
Lincoln, NE 68512
www.iuniverse.com
1-800-Authors (1-800-288-4677)

Because of the dynamic nature of the Internet, any Web addresses or links contained in this book may have changed since publication and may no longer be valid.

ISBN: 978-0-595-45152-4 (pbk)
ISBN: 978-0-595-89461-1 (ebk)

Printed in the United States of America

CONTENTS

MY HEARTFELT THANKS

Without my friends and family, both here and those that have passed over, these stories would not have been written. If I tried to name everyone who is part of the stories in this book, I would surely leave someone out and hurt feelings. Some names I never knew. Therefore, except for a few instances where I have included the names of my family and close friends, I have respected individual privacy.

I wish to thank the many priests whose words wound up in my notebook. Some I have quoted in the stories, others are a part of the journey.

My thanks go out to all that helped, both those that I have seen, and times when the help was of a different kind. I am grateful for the birds, flowers, paws, songs and other media that has been involved. It is comforting to know that I AM NOT ALONE!

IN THE BEGINNING

Soon after I was born, my mother and father moved from Chicago to a house in the country built by my father. We lived on a corner lot off the main highway on a graveled road, miles from town; a cornfield bordered our land. My maternal grandmother lived in a cinder block house at the other end of the cornfield, where the road turned. Our nearest neighbor was a quarter of a mile away.

I was already beginning to express my personality—inquisitive, determined. My parents planted fruit trees in front of our house. Wasps built a nest in one of the trees. I didn't think they belonged there and knocked the nest down with a stick. The wasps were very mad and I was the target of their anger. My mother had to rescue me, beating the wasps off with a broom.

During a Sunday afternoon drive, our car had a flat. While my father changed the tire, I wandered into a pasture to "talk to the cows." That is the reason I gave my parents when they finally found me, a tiny girl, surrounded and hidden by huge beasts.

A chicken coop was off to the side, behind the house. I didn't get the eggs everyday but when I did, the rooster would lie in wait, emerging from a dark corner to bite my legs. It didn't matter how quiet I was or how quick, he didn't like me. And I didn't like him.

After my third birthday, my brother Terry joined the family. I wanted to visit my grandmother but my mother was busy. After I made a pest of myself, she gave me permission to go if I took my brother with me. I remember walking with him to my grandma's house at the end of the lane. Halfway there, he sat down in the middle of the road and refused to move. He was tired. I couldn't carry him the rest of the way; he was too big and I wasn't big enough. Who rescued us? I don't remember.

On a cold afternoon in January, the year I was four, everything changed. My father was at work. My mother, brother and I were taking a nap in the afternoon. I woke up coughing, smoke filled the room. When I called to my mother, she picked me up and carried me out of the house. She told me to go back by the chicken coop and roll in the snow. Then she went back into the house, after my brother. Neither of them came out.

My father returned from work to learn that most of his family was gone. I had third degree burns over a large area of my body and spent a long time in the hospital. The doctors waited until I was stronger to tell me that my mother was gone.

TRACKING TIME

"Come out. Come out and play," the morning beckoned when I opened the outside door. Sunshine was everywhere, and a cloudless blue sky promised it would continue. A warm breeze teased, "no jacket needed"—a beautiful Indian summer day.

My youngest daughter, Sue, and I were at our camper, miles away from the city the second Saturday of October. Not only could I go out to play, I could spend the day outside.

Except I lost my watch the night before. I missed it as we prepared to leave the city. Our trip was delayed as I searched the house, looked everywhere without success and then looked again just in case. I didn't have another watch and it was too late to buy one.

Not having a watch wouldn't have been a bad thing on a weekend except it was Fall Festival and many events were planned. I wanted to go for the guided nature walk on the prairie at 10:00 A.M., watch the magician at noon and make a flower basket at 2:00. I knew from experience that once outside I lost track of time.

At 10:00, I drove to the prairie for the guided hike. Cars lined both sides of the road as people gathered to wander the prairie. The sun was warm; the early morning breeze rustled the leaves. Prairie grasses danced to the music, while bees visited the purple asters and sunflowers. Monarch butterflies stopped to rest among the goldenrod. Usually our leader stopped to point out the various plants, ways to identify them and herbal uses. This time was different, although she answered questions, she didn't name all the plants, instead she had a collection of poems honoring the prairie, and every so often she stopped to read one. Many times I had gone on prairie hikes, learning about the various plants and flowers. The poems were a nice addition. As I walked through the narrow pathway dwarfed by the big bluestem, I knew I needed to stay outside. When I returned from the hike, Sue took our car to the beach to meet her friends, leaving me with my blue scooter for transportation. How could I keep track of time and still stay outside? That was the question. I came up with a plan.

In September, I had enrolled in two classes at our junior college and was loaded with homework. If I put a 45-minute music tape on our tapeplayer, turned up the volume so I could hear it outside, I could do my homework at the picnic table and keep track of the time.

My plan worked perfectly. The tape ended, it was time to leave. As I prepared to put my books away, an acquaintance stopped to talk. He had a problem and needed to talk to someone. I didn't have the heart to tell him that I was leaving, so I decided to skip the magician.

When he left, I put another tape on the machine. Time passed quickly. The tape ended; once again I packed up my books. I had just gone into our trailer, when I heard someone call my name.

Looking outside, I saw our neighbor, Mary, in her truck. I was surprised to see her. Before I left for the nature hike, I watched Mary and her sister, Rowe, leave. They said they were going to help friends at their campsite and would be gone all day. Now Mary was back and seemed upset.

I was right; she was speaking so fast I had trouble understanding her.

"Is your CB working?" she called. "Rowe collapsed inside the trailer. I think she had a heart attack. The radio in our truck isn't working. I can't call anyone. Can you call security?"

I didn't want to add to the delay so I asked for their location in case I reached our campground security and told Mary to drive up to the main gate. Before Mary reached the end of her driveway, I reached security. I managed to stop her, and sent her back to her sister.

(In 1990, telephone service did not go to each campsite. Nor were cell phones widely used. Communication was by CB radio.)

Locking our trailer, I rode my scooter over to the scene of the accident. As I approached their campsite, I saw flashing lights. Help had already arrived. Emergency Medical Technicians, EMT'S were inside the small fifth wheel trailer, giving aid to Mary's sister. I didn't want to be in their way so I stood outside, talking to another friend. Her hands waved through the air as she related the events of the day. As I watched, a yellow jacket, a yellow wasp buzzed around her head. I was afraid that my friend would be stung and warned her to be careful.

She replied, "Rowe was stung today."

"Did you tell the EMT'S?" I asked.

"No", she replied.

"Don't you think you'd better?" I responded.

With that she went inside.

Only a few minutes passed before an ambulance arrived to take my neighbor to the hospital. I stayed behind to put tools away, then left for the flower arranging.

People, baskets, flowers were everywhere. The room buzzed with activity. I watched as dried flowers were poked and prodded into spaces in the baskets. Soon the instructor was at my side. "You should have come earlier," she said. "All the baskets are gone."

"That's all right," I replied. "I wasn't meant to do this today."

I watched for a while, and then rode my scooter back to our camper. As I rode, I reviewed the events of the day. First, I lost my watch. Even though I had figured out how to track time, as I prepared to leave at noon, a friend delayed me. I was still at our camper when Mary came back, looking for help. Then I noticed the yellow jacket buzzing around my friend. I realized that unseen hands had guided me to be where I needed to be so that I could be of assistance to my neighbor. Goosebumps ran up my arms when I realized that I wasn't meant to arrange flowers in a basket that day. I felt honored to be chosen.

When Mary returned from the hospital I learned that Rowe was stung seven times. Her blood sugar was very high. It wasn't her heart after all.

I was born and raised in the Catholic faith. As the years passed, months would go by without my going to Mass. Ever since that day in October, I go to Mass on weekends to say "Thank you."

QUEEN OF HEAVEN

I was born into the Roman Catholic faith. When I was in first grade, I was introduced to the world of the Sisters of St. Francis. They wore black habits that hid their legs and most of their shoes. Long veils covered their hair and ears. Sister's word was law. Daily attendance at morning Mass was expected. At each of the four grammar schools I attended, the students assembled in church for Mass before the school day began. The Blessed Virgin Mary had a very prominent place in our lives. Each school had a choir which sang not only for Sunday Masses but also for funerals and weddings. I was a member of the choir for three years. We always sang the Ave Maria when the bride took a bouquet of flowers to the Blessed Virgin. Every May, the whole school assembled for the May crowning where Mary was crowned Queen.

I had graduated from high school when Vatican II assembled in October of 1962. Many changes occurred after that assembly. The priest no longer said Mass with his back to the congregation. The Mass was said in English or the language of the country, Latin was no longer used. The nun's habits changed, they became shorter and more modern. The emphasis of the church was placed on Christ. Mary's role was played down as well as the devotions to the various saints.

After I married and began to raise my family, my attendance at Mass fluctuated. Sometimes I would attend Mass every Sunday, then I would go for months without stepping into a church. Life was busy and it was so easy to stay in bed on a Sunday morning. And time passed. I gave up formal prayer and had conversations with God instead similar to Tevya in The Fiddler On The Roof.

In 1990, I was fortunate to be in the right place at the right time. I noticed a yellow jacket circling a friend while we waited for paramedics to work on my unconscious neighbor. My words of warning reminded my friend that a wasp had stung my neighbor that day. My warning might have saved my neighbor's life. When I thought about the incident, I was honored to be chosen by God to participate and decided to go to Mass every Sunday to say "Thank You."

In 1991, the events at the cemetery on Roosevelt and Wolf Road in Hillside made the news. Miracles were reported: rosaries were turning to gold; many people were getting remarkable pictures of Jesus on the Cross. Polaroid pictures showed the Blessed Virgin Mary among the people and the doorway to heaven was also revealed. The media's attention brought many people to the cemetery. Dorothy, a friend I used to work with, invited me to go with her.

The first time I visited the cemetery, I was impressed by the peacefulness. Many people were saying the rosary. Others were standing around, looking at pictures. Stories were being told.

Another visit was planned. Dorothy and I were going to return to the cemetery and then meet another friend for lunch. I decided to go by myself when a family death prevented Dorothy from joining me. Before going back to the cemetery, I looked for an old rosary that I knew was somewhere in our house. I finally found it hidden in a box at the back of my closet. It had mother of pearl beads on a silver chain. I arrived at the cemetery just as a group began the rosary. I decided to pray for my friend and her husband. I was surprised that I had forgotten the words to the Hail Mary. It had been many years since I said them.

Dorothy accompanied me on my third visit. We were talking to a group of women when we noticed a strong aroma of roses. Without moving, we had been transported to a rose garden. We searched for the source of the fragrance without success. The bouquet of roses at the foot of the cross wasn't strong enough to give off the fragrance. No one was wearing rose perfume. That afternoon, as we were saying the rosary, sometimes I heard Dorothy's voice and sometimes I didn't. When I didn't hear her voice, I looked at her. She was staring at her rosary. After we were finished praying, Dorothy showed me her rosary. Three of her crystal beads had turned amber. I looked at my own rosary and was amazed that the silver chain was now gold. I learned later that roses are a sign that Our Lady is present.

When I told the story to others I tried to remember the name of the cemetery but it didn't matter how many times I looked at the name, it didn't stick in my brain. I finally gave up and just referred to it as the cemetery on the south side of Roosevelt at Wolf Road.

In 1994, a vendor at the crossroads where my family went camping had a large, painted statue of the Blessed Virgin Mary for sale. Whenever I stopped at the crossroads, I had a conversation with the statue. I always apologized for not buying Her, explaining that I was looking for a statue of St. Francis of Assisi because I was born on his feast day.

I attended Mass with my father in a nearby town on weekends. I couldn't remember the name of the church so I referred to it by the town's name. On any given weekend, I apologized to Mary many times.

My neighbor at the campground admired the large painted statue of Mary. Her sister decided to buy it for her birthday. My neighbor had a smaller, white statue of Mary depicting Our Lady Of Grace that came into her possession from the cemetery on the north side of Roosevelt at Wolf Rd. Since they didn't need two statues, they asked if I wanted the smaller one.

With the help of a wheel barrel, we moved the smaller statue to a place of honor in my flower garden. Our Lady's base had broken off, so we permanently dug Her into the ground. After She had been in place for over a month, I noticed that Her gown was covered with dirt. When I washed off the dirt, I noticed that part of her gown had broken off. When I fixed the broken pieces, the white statue was white and grey. My family said that as long as I was going to paint Her, I should paint Her in colors. Since She was dug into the ground, I spent quite a few hours on my hands and knees, trying to reach the many parts of the statue.

In the winter of 1997, Sue, my youngest daughter took her first plane ride to visit her sister, Terri, in Florida. The morning of her virgin flight, I attended Mass to pray for a safe trip. Since I quit work in 1995, I was a regular attendee at Friday morning Mass but I had never attended Tuesday Mass. I was surprised when after Mass, the assembly said the Devotions to Our Mother of Perpetual Help. While prayers were being said, I heard a gate close and knew that I had come home. I discovered that it was Mother Mary, in all of Her various titles, who was directing the forces that provide me with help. Soon after I learned that the cemetery on the south side of Roosevelt at Wolf was Queen of Heaven. Then I discovered that the church were I attend Mass at the camper was Our Lady Of Perpetual Help. Whatever had blocked me from remembering their names had been removed.

PAP AND THE PANCAKE TURNER

My father and I had a special relationship. After the fire, Dad and I were the only survivors of our family. When my husband and I moved back to Chicago, he invited my father to live with us, which he did until the month before he died. My children called him Pap.

Our schedules were very busy but we ate supper together as a family and breakfast on Sunday. We always knew what we were having for breakfast on Sunday morning … pancakes. Sometimes accompanied by bacon or sausage, maybe eggs. The important part of breakfast was the pancakes. They were my husband's favorite.

When my father turned 80, his memory started to decline. We thought it was just old age, but it turned out to be more than that. We didn't know it, but my father had Alzheimer's disease.

As time passed, Pap's condition quickly deteriorated. Before four years passed, Pap had forgotten much of his adult life. I was never sure if he knew that I was his daughter. Sometimes he thought I was his wife.

One of his last remaining abilities was his ability to eat. He ate with my husband, half an hour later he would eat with me, if anyone was eating soon after, he was willing to join them, because you see, he hadn't eaten in a long time and he was HUNGRY!

The month before my father died, he fell at day care. I took him to the doctor; where an EKG suggested he had a heart attack. An ambulance transferred him to the hospital where he was confined for tests for four days. In that time he forgot how to walk.

Since he couldn't walk, I couldn't take him home. He transferred from the hospital to a nursing home. While in the nursing home, I don't think he recognized me as his daughter. I was a friendly face. And if he was feeling his oats he flirted. His last words to me on Valentines Day were: "Take care of yourself, I love you." I had stopped in the nursing home to bring him a stuffed bear to keep him company. I already had a cold, which worsened as the days went by, producing a lot of phlegm. Meanwhile Pap caught a bad cold. I didn't want to give him the virus I had so I didn't see him. His condition worsened. I didn't want to expose the people at the nursing home to my germs so I didn't see him. When they phoned that he was on oxygen, I asked if he would know me if I went to visit him. They said no; he was lethargic. Since I was still sick, I didn't go to the nursing home. I wasn't there when my father died. He was only in the nursing home for a month. He passed over on Feb. 19, four days before his 85th birthday, a month after the anniversary of the fire.

The morning of my father's wake, my son Bill, my husband, Tom and I went to the pancake house for breakfast. As we waited for our order, Tom said, "Now we will be able to find things, Pap won't be taking them anymore." I answered, "Don't be too sure of that, we still have gremlins in our house." Bill piped up, "Yes, but the head gremlin is gone."

After breakfast I dropped my husband and son off at home and ran some errands. When I came back, Tom, Bill and our dogs were in the front room watching a comedy show on television. The phone rang. Tom answered it on the cordless. It was Sue, our youngest daughter. She was leaving school and wanted to know if she should pick up anything on her way home. The TV was too loud; I couldn't hear and walked into the dining room.

As I talked to her, I heard a loud clunk come from the kitchen. A question popped into my head. "What fell? No one is in the kitchen."

I have a three tier deep carousel in which I keep my kitchen gadgets on a counter. The pancake turner had fallen out of it onto the floor. "Is someone hungry?" I asked. I knew my father was sending me a message that he was all right. He remembered us.

HELP

Strange things happened in 1995, after my father's passing. Reasonable explanations can always be found if a person looks hard enough for the answer. The question is, are those reasonable explanations the answer?

My son, Bill, and Kathy, my oldest daughter, had major trouble with their computers the day of their grandfather's wake. The computers kept locking; they didn't want to work. Ivan, my youngest daughter's boyfriend, had computer trouble when he was trying to work on a school paper after the wake that evening. We figured Pap was trying the computers. He didn't have an opportunity to use them since we didn't purchase a computer until after Pap's Alzheimer's disease prevented him from learning new things.

The day of my father's memorial Mass, I brought a picture of my father, mother, brother and I and placed it in front of the altar. I hadn't been able to attend the Mass for my mother and brother when they died. Having the picture of the whole family felt right.

The resurrection choir at church gifted us with their music. One of the songs they sang is taken from Psalm 91, <u>On Eagles Wings.</u> The chorus is comforting, "And He will raise you up on eagles wings, bear you on the breath of dawn, make you to shine like the sun and hold you in the palm of His hand." But I found the fourth verse interesting, "For to His angels, he's given a command, to guard you in all of your ways ..."

After his passing, my father sent me a message that he was okay ... similar to Houdini's message to his wife. A pancake turner clunked onto the floor from the deep carousel in the empty kitchen when I was standing in the dining room. "Is someone hungry," I asked. My father did more than send a message; he let the cat out of the bag. I had always believed in life after death, but now I knew. Since the secret was out, I received more help. I was writing the story of life with Pap as his memory declined and I was very aware that I was receiving HELP as my helpers learned how to navigate via computer, a skill that Pap had never mastered.

After Pap's passing I began to seriously work on our story of living with my father as his memory declined. I tried to slow the story down, put in more details, rewrite it for the umpteenth time. My son dreamt about his grandfather—he watched him search for a black book among his things in the attic. When Bill told me about his dream, I looked for my father's black autograph book and found a reflection written by my father when he was 21 years old. I fitted his insight into the chapter that I was working on. It was almost as if my father was trying to help me.

I had been looking for a statue of St. Francis of Assisi for a long time. He is special to me not only because I was born on his feast day but because of his love of animals that we share. So I stopped at a statuary to check on statues of St. Francis. Along with his statues, they had a statue of Mary the Mother, holding a naked toddler. I liked the statue, inquired into the price and after hearing the cost, was very glad that I already had a statue of Our Lady. The owner told me that the mold for the statue had been destroyed, once it was gone, that was it.

That weekend, watching Ben, my eighteen-month grandson play, I realized I was thinking about where I was going to put the statue. I knew what statue I was thinking of; I made plans to buy the statue of Our Mother.

When I returned to the store to purchase Her, I noticed that She had fallen; her face was pushed in. When I mentioned this to the owner, he reduced the price. I took the statue to the country and tried to repair Her face.

One night I had a dream. I dreamt that I was in a very fancy, large room, like a nightclub. Men wore tuxedos and the ladies were dressed in expensive dresses, loaded with jewels and fur. They sat at white linen covered tables drinking beverages from crystal goblets. The lighting in the room was low, indirect. Music played softly in the background.

I talked to a very handsome, dark haired, slim figured man dressed in a black tuxedo. He promised me all kinds of rich, expensive things—fame, jewels, cars, clothes, trips. Whatever he wanted me to do, I didn't want to do. I kept telling him, "No, I wasn't interested."

In my dream I returned to the room the following day. It was empty, nothing was there but bare walls and floor. The furniture, rugs, fixtures were all gone. I asked myself if the man was Satan. That thought frightened me, woke me up. I didn't need his help.

In the morning I decided to have the statue of Our Mother blessed by a priest. I remembered a retired priest who lived near our camper. He was home when I arrived. I told him my story: the book and the dream. I mentioned that I had repaired Her face and still needed to paint Her, but I didn't want to wait until She was finished to have Her blessed. He agreed to bless Her, and asked if I had holy water. When I admitted that I didn't, Father Dave said he would use his but suggested that I get some and keep it on hand. He said I was lucky to find him; he had just returned from a month's trip.

When I returned to Chicago, one of my first tasks was to get a bottle of holy water. Heading for church, I stopped to talk to our school crossing guard. When I told her my story, she said that her minister had just told them to take holy water and bless their homes to chase out evil spirits. They should bless each door and window because that was the only way evil spirits could enter. Since evil spirits sometimes came in with people, the minister told them to bless the rooms regularly. When I returned to the country, I blessed every room with holy water, paying special attention to the doors.

I debated including my spiritual experiences in the story that I was writing. I decided to include them since my faith is an important part of the story.

Until I finished writing the chapter that included my experience of being guided by an invisible hand to help my neighbor, who was stung by yellow jackets, and my visit to the cemetery where my rosary turned gold, all kinds of things were happening to my computer.

Keys stuck, making me lose my train of thought. I retyped part of the chapter three times. I saved the file and the computer keys stuck, causing me to turn off the computer. My saved file was gone, never saved. I retyped the experience; I used a key to erase a word and watched as the cursor moved at breathtaking speed, erasing everything that I had written. The computer shut off by itself, before I had a chance to save what I was working on.

After I wrote my experiences in that chapter, I didn't have as much trouble with the computer until I decided to write the story of how I got the statue of Our Lady that sits in my garden at the camper. Once again, mischief occurred in major fashion to my computer.

I was very concerned that I might lose all of my work. I kept three separate disks containing my files. One disk I used for current work, another I used as a back up at the camper, and a third that I updated whenever I returned home. For further protection, I printed a revised hard copy often.

Vacation time—my husband and I headed for Cherokee, North Carolina. On the way we stopped at the Holy Ghost church in Knoxville, Tennessee. After Mass, I took the opportunity to take pictures of the beautiful church, it's old-fashioned altar railings and beautiful windows. One of the ushers noticed my activities and stopped to talk to us. He said that when he and his wife moved to Knoxville, their protestant neighbors asked if they came to convert them. He replied, "We came to LOVE you." (Years later, I met the tall usher again. He was the father of one of the priests at our church. Small world!)

While we were in Cherokee, I met an Indian man near a stream of water, who was sitting on the bed of his truck, making wooden flowers from branches and giving them to the children. While he carved the wood, he shared his culture and thoughts with them. I was fascinated by his skill and joined the group. We got into a discussion. He thought living in a city polluted a person. I didn't agree. While I loved the mountains and clean water, I thought it was possible to live in a city and not be corrupt. I told him that we lived in Chicago and I didn't feel polluted. I still have the wooden flower he gave me.

Returning from vacation, we stopped for dinner at a restaurant. Continuing our drive, we decided to look for a motel room for the night. It was the Fourth of July weekend; the motels were filled. Then it started to rain. While we drove toward home, I tried to raise the electric passenger side window, it was stuck, it wouldn't go up. My husband tried, his button wouldn't work either.

We continued our search for a motel room, driving another 40 miles. At the next town, after being told that there was no room at the inn, I asked where in town we might find an open room. Four motels were booked; we should try the fifth. They had a room and gave us a bag and tape to protect our open window, which still wouldn't close. In the morning, the passenger side window went up.

Heading for the camper after vacation, I absent-mindedly placed my glasses on the roof of my car. While I was traveling through a twenty-mile-per-hour speed zone in town, I heard a thump. Looking out my side view mirror, I saw a small brown case on the road behind me. Parking my car, I walked back, staying directly in front of my glasses so the approaching car wouldn't run over them. I was going to the camper for three weeks with my granddaughter; I would not have been able to continue to write without my glasses.

One of the advantages of staying at the camper was swimming in the pool on a hot day. While my granddaughter was with me, I spent more time in the water. One afternoon I got into a discussion with Barbara, a Pottawatomie Indian princess. We discussed life after death and a person's inheritance. As the daughter of an Indian chief, she felt she should have inherited a large piece of land. I replied that no matter what a person inherited, they were responsible to make the best use of the talents that they had received; they shouldn't rest on the laurels of their ancestors. Barbara decided that I was Indian, white people don't speak as I do. I disagreed, I knew my ancestry. My father was a full-blooded Swede and my mother's parents were from Germany and Ireland. Barbara insisted I was Indian. I couldn't convince her that I wasn't so I finally agreed that since our ancestors traveled so much, I could have Indian blood. Before summer ended, my friend Rosie gave me an Indian name, "fart on the wind," because I never stayed home.

My son came out to the camper, bringing his laptop computer. He asked if I wanted to use it. He said his computer had a color monitor, was faster, easier to use.

Bill told me of the dreams he was having about his grandfather, roaming through the house, looking for something. He said he brought Pap with him. I think he did; Bill didn't have any more trouble. I had more interesting things happen.

I tried to use Bill's computer. It wouldn't let me; a message appeared saying that the drive needed to be reconfigured. Nothing I tried worked. When my son returned the next weekend, he fixed it. The next time I turned his computer on, it gave me more strange messages. I turned it off, took holy water and blessed the camper again. Then I took my computer and wrote the story of how I got the statue of Our Lady that is in our garden.

I figured out how to work with my notebook computer. It had strange character flaws that added interest to writing. The direction keys stuck, inserting numbers, the keyboard froze in the shift position, sometimes I could get it unstuck, sometimes I had to turn the computer off and start all over again. I tried to save my work often to guard against such happenings.

If the computer was really acting up, I shut it off and did something else for a while. One morning, I wanted to write for a couple of hours, then I planned to see a friend. My computer keys were sticking, the shift keys were getting stuck, and sentences were erasing themselves. Mischief was afoot, lots of mischief. I explained to whomever would listen—wind, birds, spirits—that I was only going to work for an hour, then visit my friend. The computer behaved, before a half-hour passed, my friend visited me.

I was alone in the camper, working on my story. The space saving, hanging spice cabinet opened by itself in the kitchen, spices fell all over the floor.

That week, a knock woke me at 4:40 A.M. from a sound sleep. I looked outside; no one was there. It wasn't the knocking of a bird or animal, but the rhythmic sound of human hands.

When I told my friends about the week's experiences, they asked if I blessed the camper. Of course, I had, after the knock, before going back to bed.

The following day, as I vacuumed the rugs, I started laughing. I realized that my father was with me. I told him that he didn't need to knock on a door to come in; he was a spirit now. If it wasn't my father but the other one, he wasn't welcome.

I rewrote chapter, upon chapter. When I reread what I had written, it called for a rewrite. I rewrote a story about my grandson's first birthday, expanding the story. My computer played games: stuck numbers, stuck shift key, sticking keys, deleting words and sentences. I gave up, rebooted the computer and wrote something else. The computer worked perfectly as if I wasn't supposed to be writing about my grandson. Later, after reflecting on the story, I agreed.

As I headed back to the city down a country road, I slowed my car to avoid hitting an animal. The animal was low to the ground with a white stripe down its head. After it moved past my car, it turned around to hiss at my tires. I thought it was a badger. When I arrived home, I looked up badgers in *Animal Speaks*, a book about animals written by Ted Andrews. I was right. The animal was a badger. I was surprised to learn that the badger was a keeper of stories. I thought his crossing my path when I was writing a story about living with my father was appropriate. When I arrived back in the country, I told others about my encounter. I learned that I had a very unique experience. No one I talked to had ever seen a badger and they had lived in the country all their lives.

While in the city, I visited Transitions, an independent bookstore. I was surprised to see a Lakota Sundancer; an Indian woman dressed in bright yellow, in traditional Indian garments, giving a lecture. I didn't know an author was scheduled to speak. Mary Thunder had just finished her presentation when I arrived. She passed around a chalice filled with water from Lourdes. When it came to me, I dipped my hand in and blessed myself. When the author passed by me, she asked if I had gotten what I came for. I was surprised by her question, it sounded like she had expected me, knew I was coming.

It was a beautiful fall day in October at the campground, a perfect day for a walk, a scooter ride, and raking leaves, burning branches if the wind died down. I went for a walk. It was still windy when I returned, so I went for a scooter ride. I stopped by a friends house and was offered lunch, I refused since I dropped in for appetizers the day before. I returned to our camper.

After eating lunch, the wind was so gusty that a fire was risky. Our fire pit wasn't deep enough. Rain was expected along with falling temperatures. I wanted to burn the branches but I didn't want to burn our camper. I took the scooter for another ride. It wasn't windy in other parts of the park. I went down to the wetland area, walked the trails, and climbed the new bird observation tower. Enjoyed the day. I felt that someone didn't want me to work.

I decided to stop at the country store for an ice cream cone. I got a piece of strawberry rhubarb pie too.

Clouds were coming in; the temperature was starting to drop. I decided to return to our lot. I wasn't sure what to do. Maybe burn the branches, maybe break them up and put them in bags and store them inside until better weather.

There were too many branches to break up, to put in bags. It was still windy, gusty. I decided that I would get everything that I needed: gloves, matches, rake, jacket, something to drink. I would turn on the water hose. I would stand guard over the fire so it wouldn't spread.

That is what I did. I raked the leaves that were close by, kept the fire low, raked more leaves, added them to the low fire, and kept this up until the sky darkened again. I decided to let the fire burn down. I stirred, lifted the leaves, and smoothed the top. The wind took embers for a ride. I used the hose to drench the outer circle. Stirred, lifted and smoothed. The smoke started chasing me around the fire. It didn't matter in which direction I moved, the smoke was there. I explained to the world in general that I was afraid to leave the fire; the wind was still spreading the embers. I raked, stirred, lifted and smoothed, chased by the smoke. It started to rain; I put everything inside except for the rake and the hose. I got my umbrella and watched the fire. As the rain became heavier, I put away our good rake and used a broken one to lift and stir, watched embers fly in the wind, still chased by the smoke.

The sky continued to darken; rumbling was heard in the distance. I watched the fire, the embers and the sky. My umbrella closed by itself. I gave up, turned off the water and went inside. As soon as I closed the door, the sky opened, dumping buckets of water in seconds.

Although I had a printer at the camper, I printed most of my rewrites on my printer at home. Whenever I printed chapter three I knew I would have trouble—the printer jammed, or the paper would crinkle and tear or the ribbon would print on the same line over and over and over again. I knew the exact spot where the problem would surface, Terri's housewarming party. Our middle daughter had just bought a small house in the suburbs and invited the family and friends to celebrate. I wanted to include the party because it showed my father's memory loss in a lighthearted way.

Thunderstorms were predicted the day of the party, which Terri planned to hold in her big backyard. In early afternoon strong winds blew the clouds away and sunshine and blue skies followed. It turned into a beautiful day.

Each time the printer objected, I rewrote the story. I perked coffee, sizzled hot dogs and hamburgers on the grill, roasted the chicken on a spit, then browned it. Then deleted descriptions the next time it jammed.

I was perplexed. I couldn't figure out the problem. I didn't think the story was objectionable, it was cute. My father wanted to go home with his sisters; he forgot he was going with me. The printer had fits each time I printed chapter three, not only for weeks or months but years.

In 2002, print on demand publishing received a lot of publicity. Information and ads on television turned up everywhere. I finally gave in and decided to self publish with iuniverse. The printer was still jamming whenever I tried to print chapter three, at the spot of the party. It printed the pages before and after without a problem. I was concerned that every time the book was printed, chapter three would jam. I had to solve the problem.

The solution finally percolated through my brain. I realized I was missing the point. There wasn't anything wrong with the descriptions of the party; I missed the gift we received—the gift of a beautiful day. After I made that discovery, printing chapter three was no problem at all.

FEATHERS

A black feather fell as I was sitting outside at the picnic table, drinking my morning cup of coffee before leaving for church to attend mass on the feast of the Assumption Of Our Lady.

It was a gray day, foggy, damp, cool. The coolness was welcome after the heat we experienced during the summer, the grey fog was not. I needed the sun; my mood sometimes reflected the brightness or dreariness of the day.

I watched the feather slowly float down. The prior owner was gone, nowhere to be seen. The feather reminded me of the feather that floated down from the dove as a message from Holly, to her daughter, that she had received her angel's wings in the movie A Message From Holly.

I realized how important feathers had become to me this summer. Both on and off the owner. At times when I have been very sad, I have noticed a bird that cheered me up.

During the spring, my husband told me that he could always tell when I was home. There were more birds outside, sitting on the fences, flying around. I thought he was just teasing me, but now I wasn't so sure.

Writing our story at the camper, without my family around, has been difficult. Many of the events dragged down my spirit, left me feeling very heavy. Often, I wanted a hug but there was no one around. I wasn't going to ask a friend for a hug. I didn't want to try to explain my request. I couldn't call my family every time I got lonely or depressed, it was too expensive. During those times, I was often surprised by feathers.

They weren't just commonplace birds; they were unique visitors that I didn't see daily. A bluebird sat on a branch on one of the trees in front and serenaded me. Another day, a bluebird stopped for a bath in our muddy ditch. (I was low on money but I went and bought it a birdbath.)

A different day, I returned from a walk to see a Baltimore oriole perched in the tree above our blackberry canes. I have never seen a Baltimore oriole at our lot in the twenty years we have owned it. This year they visited on two different occasions, each time when my spirit was heavy, staying long enough to sing a song for me.

I finished rewriting a hard chapter and went outside to shake off the gloom. Sitting in one of our trees, I saw a beautiful red tail hawk. It lingered only a few minutes before it flew off to continue hunting.

Walking back from a friend's, I reflected on our conversation. We were discussing her involvement with "Rainbow Kids", children from broken homes. She told me that the guidebooks didn't cover all the situations that arose; she often had to rely on her own judgment and hope that it was right. I told her that no book could cover everything. As I walked, I realized that I couldn't cover all the different situations in our story that other people would experience dealing with their loved one who had mental dementia. All I could do was to write honestly about what my family had experienced.

As I rounded the bend in the road, I looked up to see a hawk on the telephone pole. It stretched its wings so that I could get a good view. It waited on the pole until I returned with my camera, but flew away before I got close enough to take a picture.

Hummingbirds have appeared at our feeder when I have been sad. They have hovered close enough to the screen door so that I could admire their beautiful colors. The red on the bird's throat was a neon red, brighter, more brilliant than the red syrup in the feeder. Their young have peered in our screen door to see what I was doing. As I sat at the far side of the picnic table so as not to disturb them, they flew to my side to say thank you for the cool, fresh syrup I put out for them.

I heard a screech owl one evening as I worked on a particularly difficult passage. It's call sounded like it was coming from the hill behind our camper. My friends had told me that it was in their trees at night but I hadn't heard it.

I looked out the window at our bird feeder and noticed a blackberry leaf bobbing in the wind. The leaf was wearing a feather like a woman wears a hat. On closer inspection, I found a blue jay's feather piercing the leaf like a sword through a piece of paper.

Sitting in our recliner, I edited the chapter dealing with my father's hospital confinement. I noticed a purple finch flapping it's wings as if trying to land on the window, then landing in a branch of a nearby tree. It returned to the window to flap its wings, then returned to the tree. It was passed breeding season, I was puzzled by it's behavior. I had just refilled our bird feeder; it couldn't be trying to tell me it was hungry. Then I noticed the squirrel sitting on our bird feeder. I guess it was trying to tell me that it was hungry.

"Remember the birds and flowers are not greater than you and they are cared for."

THE VOICES

I wrote this as an exercise for Creative Writing. We were supposed to write in a different style so I used my imagination. My life had already changed considerably. I received more "help" than I ever dreamed possible. My "friends in high places" as I was beginning to call them, often woke me up at 4:00 AM. When my father was alive, he thought he could think better at that time of day. He even set his alarm so he would wake up. His sister Connie also got up that early. She had become another of my "friends in high places". I thought getting up at seven was early enough. To make matters worse, an itch had developed on both of my ankles. Scratching it felt better than eating chocolate or ice cream. Imagine if you will, three or four angels sitting around, conniving. The events are true. The dialogue is fiction. Or is it?

"She is awake. She should be up!"

"How are we going to get her out of bed? Nothing is working. She looks at the clock, rolls over, buries her head in the pillow and lays there."

"It is after 6:00. Time is flying, she is wasting the day."

"She ignores all the ideas we give her. Tells her brain to shut up, go back to sleep. Rolls over. Lays there."

"I made her pillow lumpy, it didn't work. She rolled over."

"The dogs want to sleep too. I tried to get them to tell her that they wanted to go out. They ignored me. They don't want to get up this morning."

"It wouldn't do any good anyway. He closed their bedroom door when he left."

"If they barked or whined she would get up."

"But they didn't get up. They can sleep; she is the one who has to get up. How are we going to get her up?"

"I know! I know! I know how we can do it!"

"You're so smart. How?"

"We can make her itch."

"So we make her itch. She scratches, then she lies there."

"That's because you're not doing it right."

"What do you mean I'm not doing it right? There is not a right way and a wrong way to make someone itch."

"Oh yes there is. I can make her itch so she gets up."

"Oh yeah!"

"Yeah"

"So, smarty. How are you going to do it?"

"I'm going to start out with just a little itch. She will scratch it, just a little bit, then roll over. I'll wait a couple of minutes; let her think that the itch is gone. Then I'll make it itch just a little bit more. After she scratches, I'll take the itch back for a couple of minutes. Give her a false sense of security. Then I'll make her itch again. This time I'll make a bigger spot itch, and maybe add another place. Spread it around a little bit. She won't notice that the itch is growing. She still wants to sleep. This time I won't wait as long after she scratches to make the itch come back. She will only be scratching her ankle. Now I will add her calf, just one spot, along with her ankle. I'll make it feel really good to scratch, so she scratches longer, really gets into it. Now I'll wait only a second before adding her foot to her ankle, along with her calf. Itch, Itch, Itch. She won't be able to lie there. She will have to get up."

"Go ahead and try it. What have we got to lose? She is just lying there. She will lie there all day. She doesn't have a job, she doesn't think she needs to get up."

"She never lays there all day. We have seen to that."

"All right, so she won't lay there all day, just until 7:00."

"She is awake. We woke her up. We gave those people something to say right outside her window at 5:00."

"We made those tires stick to the road so all they did was spin and squeal. We made her listen to the traffic on the street. Made her think that there was a lot of snow on the ground."

"She didn't get out of bed to look."

"But we woke her up."

"Now we have to get her on her feet. Out of bed. In motion."

"The itch will do it."

"You think so."

"I know so!"

"Try it. What have we got to lose?"

"Told you so. Told you so. The itch did it. Not even 15 minutes. She is up. She is dressed. She is in motion."

"Did you watch carefully? Take notes. So we can do it again tomorrow."

REFLECTIONS

It is a beautiful Fall morning—jacket weather, the sun is shining, the wind is very brisk. I sketch my day in my mind as I walk, admire the colors of the leaves, listen to the birds, reflect on my life.

The road curves, hiding from view what is to come. My life is often like the road, curving, hidden from view. Sometimes the road that I travel seems to be very straight, I can see for miles, it seems smooth, even boring. The smoothness can be deceptive—often, a sudden dip or a hole causes delay, problems. Just as a car gets a flat tire or breaks down causing trouble, unexpected events, health problems, loss of jobs, unexpected repairs change the smoothness of my road. Sometimes I meet a new friend or an old one, causing me to pause, to stop, to detour or to change directions.

Today, I am walking in the opposite direction, going a different way, traveling the same road, backwards. Looking at things from a different angle, I see things I haven't noticed before. Looking at my life in reverse, I can clearly see my journey except where the road is hidden by fog.

While I was preparing for my speech, How I Overcame Shyness, I looked at my life in detail, analyzed it to see what had changed me from a shy person to the person I am today. I realized how much help I had received, how my step was guided, each job prepared me for the next one. I gradually overcame my shyness, gained confidence, became a leader, prepared for the next part of my journey.

Many of the courses that I have taken in school were taken at the appropriate time, when I needed them. I studied psychology at the time my father's loss of memory was starting to become a problem. I took a Saturday class at the time I needed to remain in the city on weekends. I learned that a creative writing class was offered at school after my daughter told me that I should write our story. The books that I am reading for Creative Writing are following an order that was not designed by me but are appearing when I need them to help me with the next step in my writing.

One of my life goals has not been to write an article, story or a book. I have always admired paintings, the ability to draw. I wished that I could paint but didn't think that I had the talent. My early attempts at drawing didn't meet with success.

I never wished that I could write. I enjoy reading a good book but I knew that I did not have the talent nor the imagination to write myself. So here I am, being pulled, kicking, screaming, by the hair, arm, toenails to write our story.

Before writing class, I discussed with a classmate my lack of imagination. I told her that I didn't have one and if I ever did, it was gone, replaced by practical common sense.

During class, the subject of imagination arose. Creative Writing class is a class for the imagination. Now I knew the reason that I have so much trouble with images. No imagination.

The chapter in the book by Brenda Ueland that I am currently reading is dealing with imagination. "And presently your soul gets frightfully sterile and dry because you are so quick, snappy and efficient about doing one thing after another that you have not time for your own ideas to come in and develop and gently shine."

I know why I am writing our story; I don't need an imagination to create the details of the story. A functioning memory would be a great help. One of my regrets at the moment is that I didn't take better notes, write down the little things, keep the letters I wrote to my daughter. But I don't want to focus on my regrets.

Looking back, the fog on my road is very thick at times. I don't remember many details of the years when my children were small. Looking back through the fog is like standing at the bottom of a steep, snowy hill with a sled. I know I took the ride, had some fun along with the bumps but it was quickly over.

Last year at this time, I was shackled by a job that was hazardous to my physical and mental health. I was tied down by responsibilities to my father. I could not look ahead, to see what was coming and did not want to look back. I only had the energy to focus on the next step, and after that, the next step, believing that somehow I would survive.

What a difference a year makes. My father is no longer my responsibility—I don't have a job. This year I'm broke, learning how to be a bum. FREE! Free to wander, to write, to paint, to recover. A friend told me that it took her four years before she returned to normal after caring for her husband who had Alzheimer's. I don't want to wait four years. But knowing the length of time that it took someone else might help me to have patience with myself. I think that I am fine, then dissolve into tears for no reason. I have noticed that this summer I have gone out of my way to avoid conflict, arguments, discord, confrontation. I don't feel that I have the strength to wage battles, to fight, to become upset.

A friend told me that as a person grows older, their faith should grow also. Mine has been growing without my knowledge for quite some time. Looking back, I can see the events that contributed to its growth. Looking ahead, I know that help will be available when I need it. I also know that I need all the help that I can get.

I have gone on a journey this summer without ever getting into a car, train or plane. Before this summer, I knew that I received help for big things: a young man drove by on a country road and stopped to change my tire; my car died next to a farmhouse, the farmer drove me back to the camper; a man came by in a truck to pull my car out of a ditch. This year I realized that I receive help daily, for the small things, that I have been receiving this help for many years but was too busy to notice.

This knowledge gives me a sense of comfort. It is almost as if I have an automatic pilot that I can switch on when I am tired. Of course, my confidence level is always much higher when the road is smooth, the trick will be to keep it high when the road is bumpy or is lost from sight because of the fog.

Looking ahead, the road is interesting, curves sharply, hides what lies ahead. Will the road continue to curve or will I go around a bend to find that it has straightened again?

THE PROJECT

My father was an inventive person. He had an imaginative, creative mind. I am not like my father.

My father was very skilled with his hands; he was a good craftsman, a skilled carpenter. I am not like my father.

Our family expanded. We needed more room, so Dad turned the attic into a usable space, which he used for his bedroom and workshop.

My father noticed that the only access to our roof was via the roof of the apartment house next door. Their building was built on the property line. Our roof butts up to their bricks. In order to clean the leaves out of our gutters or any other roof maintenance, we climbed their stairs, pulled down their ladder, opened their hatch, climbed over the edge of their roof and dropped down to ours. We reversed the process on the descent.

In order to give us ready access to our roof, my father cut a hatch into our roof. He framed the inside hole and constructed a cover, which fit like a hat. The hatband was wood, the covering itself made of metal, which kept out the rain, snow, and cold.

My father's memory declined. He was no longer vigilant and didn't notice needed repairs. Overtime the pieces of the hatband under the metal had decayed, letting in the rain, snow and cold. Then my father died.

We were totally ignorant of the problem until in the spring when we noticed a puddle of water on a bedroom floor. We tracked the water to its source and saw gray sky through the edges of the hatch cover; the wood in the hatband had decayed. Temporarily, we stuffed plastic bags into the hole to stop the rain from coming in.

Spring passed, followed by summer. No repairs were made to the hatch. Fall arrived, soon to be followed by winter. My husband was working long hours. When he came home from work, he was too tired to attempt the job. Although he is skilled in many areas, carpentry wasn't one of them.

I knew something had to be done, the hatch cover needed to be repaired.

On a beautiful Monday morning in early November, I decided to try to make the repairs. Unlocking the cover, I lifted it off the frame onto the roof, turned it around and maneuvered it inside. The outer surface of the cover was metal, bent and pounded into the shape of a lid for the box. The interior, the lining of the lid was constructed of two pieces of plywood, framed by uprights on all four sides. The wood supported the metal, helping it to keep its shape.

Close observation indicated that two of the uprights had decayed. The board at the top and the one to the west had suffered from the weather, crumbling into bits and pieces. Both needed to be replaced. How much skill would be needed?

I couldn't hammer a nail straight into wood, they always bent. I couldn't saw a straight line. I didn't have wood working skills but I had determination and the need to fix the cover. I thought I could replace two boards. How hard would it be?

I measured the boards that had decayed. The top board was 1 ½" thick and 25" long. The side board was only 1 ¼" inches thick but 32" long.

We had wolmanized lumber scraps in our basement, salvaged from our new porch. I went on a hunt, searching to see what I could find. Everything was 2" thick. Finally I found a couple of scraps that were thinner. Then I realized I forgot to measure the width. Back upstairs to the attic. The width on the old lumber was 3". Down to the basement, no scraps were 3" wide, everything was wider. Hunting through the nooks and crannies, I didn't find any usable timber. Back up to the attic to continue the search. I was starting to feel like a yo-yo, down and up, three flights of stairs, down and up. I decided to go to a lumber company and buy the size I needed.

At the lumberyard, I explained my requirements to the salesman and learned they didn't have the size I needed either. They didn't carry wood 1 ½" thick, nor did they have 1 ¼" thick. The industry standard was 1" or 2". Neither would work on our hatch. How nice! Now what? The salesperson suggested a lumber company that handled odd size wood.

I drove home, deciding to use a piece of lumber that was 1 ½" thick and 12" wide. I would just cut off a 3" piece. Then I would cut it down to 25". Simple. Right!

I measured, I drew my lines, I found a saw. I couldn't find an electric saw, so I had to use muscle power. Then I tried different levels and places to saw. I remembered seeing my father kneel on the piece of wood he was sawing. What could I put the board on so I could kneel on it and still cut it? I looked for his old green stool. It was gone. Searching again, I found an old roofing tar can, it was big enough, the right height. Positioning the piece of lumber on the can, I put a knee on it to hold it steady and started to saw. I don't have strength in my wrist. Using both hands I made some progress, slowly, slowly, very slowly I inched my way down the line. Every so often, I stopped to rest … my back … my hands … my knee. The saw was starting to bind. I turned the board around to saw from the other side, slowly … very slowly. When the saw started to bind I reversed the board again. Eventually my two sawed lines met; finally I was able to cut a somewhat uneven 3" piece. All I had to do was cut it down to 25". The saw didn't want to cut the board, it wanted to stick. In desperation, I tried breaking it. Now it was uneven. That's what I get for being impatient. Down and up the stairs again. Searching for a file, looking for sandpaper, looking for anything that would smooth the wood.

I tried to remove the rotted top board from the frame. It was nailed into place through the metal. Some of the nails were easy to remove, almost falling out, then there were the rest. Using the head of the hammer and a screwdriver to get under the nail head to try to pry it up, I managed to remove all but one. I couldn't budge it. I tried to use the screwdriver to pry the wood off the frame. A piece gave way. I discover that my father had pieced the top board, used two pieces of wood to make one. The remaining little piece was wedged in very tightly. It did not want to leave the frame. Carefully, so as not to damage the frame, I pried from the top … from the bottom … from the side … from the end. I finally freed it from the nail that was holding it in place. Then I was able to get the nail out.

Relieved to finally be making progress, I picked up the piece of lumber I cut and tried to put it into the empty space but it didn't fit. It was too thick. Getting the measuring tape, I measured the old pieces. The bigger piece of wood was 1 ½" thick, the smaller piece only 1 ¼"; I measured the wrong piece.

I was frustrated and worse off then when I had started. The temperature dropped, the wind picked up, the sky darkened. A storm approached. I replaced the cover, found more plastic to stuff in the bigger empty space, put buckets underneath and called it a day.

Tuesday morning was a beautiful day, blue sky, warm temperatures. I drove to the lumber company that carried different size lumber. The salesperson explained that I was in the wrong place, they only carried hard wood. If I used their wood, it would warp. I should go to a regular lumber company and purchase the wood. When I explained they didn't have the size I needed, I learned that if I bought the wood from them, they would plane it for me, cut it to the thickness I needed.

I thought of a skilled carpenter I knew. I seriously considered asking for his help. He was extremely busy, so I decided to try to fix it one more time.

I went to Handy Andy lumber company. I bought a piece of wolmanized lumber 1" x 4" x 6'. I looked for foam rubber to stick in the empty space. I saw a sign "Let Handy Andy cut your wood for you." I liked that idea. The lady at the checkout counter said the first piece cut was free, the next cost 50 cents. I couldn't pass up that deal. Save my hands, save my arm … knees … back. Worked for me.

I walked back to get my lumber cut, only to learn they didn't cut treated wood. (When a lumber company doesn't cut it, you know you are in trouble.) They said they cut other lumber, but only crosswise, not lengthwise. I could cut it crosswise.

Home again, back to square one. I removed and emptied the bucket, removed the dripping plastic bags, unlocked the cover and brought it back inside. This time I measured in more than one place. I decided to cut the wood 2 ¾" wide, just in case. The 1" thick wood I bought was only ¾" thick, industry standard.

I measured, marked 2 ¾" and drew lines. I measured 25" and drew a line and measured 32" more. I placed the wood on the pail and started to saw. I told myself it would be easier, the wood was thinner. I sawed and took a break and sawed some more. It was not easier. I took a coffee break and then sawed some more. This time I couldn't saw from the other end. I didn't want the whole 72" when I only needed 57". I made progress but slowly, oh so slowly. I tried to support the part that had been sawed so the saw wouldn't get stuck. I tried to remember the best way to use a saw, I couldn't remember if I ever knew. Finally I reached my first line at 25". I sawed passed the line, determined to free the first piece. The saw did not want to cut crosswise. I hadn't gone very far, maybe an inch when the saw stuck, it wouldn't move. I tried sawing from the other side; I made a little progress but nothing to brag about. Now I knew why the lumber company wouldn't cut it. Finally my 25" piece was free. Only one more piece to go.

I sawed and sawed. To break the monotony, I tried to free the 32" piece from the frame. My father used screws and one nail to keep that piece of wood attached to the metal. Again, some of the screws were loose and easily removed, then there were the rest. He used different size screws. I had to find different size screwdrivers.

My father was an inventive person, resourceful. I am not like my father.

I sawed and sawed … slowly … slowly … inching my way down the lumber. I twisted and turned the screws, trying to get them to release their hold. I pried and pried, coaxing the nail out. Finally I freed the rotted piece of wood from the frame; finally I reached the 32" mark.

I still had to cut the piece crosswise. The piece did not want to be cut. In the process of moving the wood, I knocked a framed, heavy picture of the Sacred Heart of Jesus off the wall, hitting my head, turning my hair red. I saw stars. Whatever patience I had left was gone. I protested loudly to the dust and the wood. Tears running down my check, I explained that I was doing the best that I could and would appreciate help. Being hit on the head was not the help that I needed.

More determined than ever, I tried to separate the piece I needed from the rest. Finally free, the edge was very uneven. It didn't fit. I tried to cut off more, it didn't work. File in hand, I took off more, that barely worked.

Meanwhile, the beautiful day had disappeared, replaced by gray skies and a cool wind that puffed its way into the attic at every opportunity. I tried to block the wind's entrance, but that cut off my light source.

Before nailing my new piece of wood to the frame, I decided to see if the cover would fit on the hatch. It didn't. I thought about going out onto the roof to get a better look, but our roof was slanted. I would need a ladder to get back into the hatch or I would be stranded outside until someone came home. I didn't want to be stuck outside with the temperature dropping. I decided to solve the problem from inside.

I discovered that the problem was the 25" piece of wood, the side that I had sawed twice. The original had been 3" wide but because it rotted away, we had filled the space with roofing tar. There wasn't room for 3" now.

I tried the 1 ¼" piece I had left from the original cut. It wasn't wide enough; there wasn't room to nail it. I started searching again. Down and up. I thought that somewhere in our house, a piece of wood 25" long, 2" wide and 1" thick must have been hiding. Outside, under the porch, I found a pole I used in the garden for pole beans. It was much easier to cut than the wolmanized lumber. I didn't know what kind of wood it was but I didn't care. It fit. The cover fit. With foam weather-stripping, the cover might be water, snow, and rain resistant.

The nails I bought were too long. The tacks I bought were too short. The roofing nails I bought were too big to go through the metal. I didn't want to use screws.

My father was resourceful; he was a pack rat. He kept many things. I am like my father.

I found a container full of odd assorted nails, scrounged from this and that. I found enough nails to do the job. I nailed them in. Some went in easy, some did not, they didn't always go in straight. The weather-stripping was put in place. I put the cover back on and latched it. I was finished.

My father was stubborn, determined to finish a task. I am like my father.

FALL FESTIVAL 1996

In March of 1996, I was still working on *To Pap, with Love* and trying to find a publisher without success. With each rejection I wondered if the story was supposed to be published.

While I was trying to learn how to write, I attended a Christ Renews His Parish weekend for women at our Catholic Church. I felt I should go but I didn't know why. Most of the women who attended were returning to their faith; I was firm in mine. I had gotten into the habit of talking to my friends in high places similar to the father in <u>Fiddler on the Roof</u>. I kept asking, "Why am I here? Am I supposed to help someone?" As the time passed, I listened to the stories of many women, each illustrating how God was active in her life. Then it became clear to me that I had a few areas to work on myself. Although I was no longer shy, I kept my faith to myself. A new question surfaced—Would I be able to talk openly about my beliefs? The last song of the weekend was <u>Be Not Afraid</u>. My question was answered when my songbook opened to the exact page: "Be Not Afraid, I go before you. Come follow me and I will give you rest." New questions surfaced— Follow You where? Rest from what?

Our assignment when we finished the weekend was to write a personal commitment before our next gathering. Early on a rainy morning at the camper on Palm Sunday, March 31, Gramma Witting's birthday, I decided to try to write it. This is what I came up with:

> We have to do our fair share on this earth to help. My fair share might be out
> in the world with the book, reaching out to those who are being worn down

taking care of a loved one. With over four million or billion already afflicted with mental dementia and the number rising, that is a lot of reaching out.

Since I don't talk the talk, quoting scripture, I might be able to reach more people. I might also be dismissed as a religious nut or just a nut.

The page I opened to in the bible at CHRP is possibly a hint of what is to come. I don't remember the exact words but it dealt with treating the older people with respect, as your parents, and the younger people as your brothers or sisters—with respect.

I thought it was appropriate at the time and didn't look for another passage. I didn't realize the full significance of those words until now.

All I need to know is that with God, all things are possible. "Be not afraid, I go before you. Come follow me and I will give you rest." With God all things are possible, taking care of a person with mental dementia, surviving an impossible job, getting through a difficult day, finding a new job or **GOING OUT INTO THE WORLD TO PROMOTE A BOOK—or PHILOSOPHY OF LIFE.**

After I wrote my personal commitment, I went for my normal three-mile walk in the light rain. I crossed the damn and the spillway. I had my umbrella, I was protected from the rain, or so I thought. A car passed by, hitting a pothole, drenching me with water—pants, jacket, face, hair—dripping. I laughed and told the rain that I was already baptized. As I turned the corner, a strong wind came up, turning my umbrella inside out. What's this, I joked. Are you handing me a towel. A friend commented later that the wind was the Holy Spirit. I thought that I had been confirmed. Now I know the date that I was rebaptized and confirmed.

When I went to the CHRP weekend, I thought it would only take up one weekend of my time. I didn't know that the participants met regularly to follow a program so they could sponsor the next CHRP weekend.

The focus of the program was to discover how God was working in our lives and then share that knowledge with others. Each participant chose a subject from a list, then prepared a talk illustrating the theme. After some reflection I chose community. Throughout my life so many people—family, friends, doctors, nurses, policeman, and strangers—had been there for me when I needed help.

After one meeting, I was very depressed when I returned home. The speaker for the evening had lost her husband in a robbery three years before. At the end of the evening, it was very apparent that she was stuck in that tragedy. We couldn't help her nor could we get her to talk about the current events in her life.

Arriving home, I was drained. I didn't want to eat, nor did I want anything to drink. I found myself sighing uncontrollably. In desperation I randomly opened the bible to the story of Jesus walking on the water. After I digested the story, I realized I couldn't help or solve every problem. I couldn't walk on water but I could give the problem to the One who could.

I felt a little better but not ready for bed. I opened an issue of Guidepost magazine to a story about a family's struggle with a tornado. Since I had enough destruction for one evening, I flipped to another. I read a short story about a man contemplating suicide who was saved by a friend's visit. After they spent some time talking, life didn't look as bad. At an AA meeting the following week, he learned that his friend had also been thinking of taking his own life, but was also saved by their conversation.

I realized I had received another reason to publish *To Pap, With Love*. Reading my family's struggle with Alzheimer's might help someone else.

Feeling better I read the next story. A woman no longer visited her favorite nature area because it had become a dumping ground. Her niece fondly remembered the place and wanted to visit again. When the aunt reluctantly took her, the girl found beautiful wild flowers growing in the nick and crannies of the trash.

I decided to look for the beauty when I heard sad or troubling stories. Then give the problem to God. Feeling better, I was able to go to bed.

One of the highlights of the CHRP weekend was letters from our families and friends telling us how important we were in their lives. A sponsor gave each of us a specially designed computer card. I was so impressed with the card, I decided to make my own cards for the weekend that our group would sponsor in the Fall.

On a beautiful Indian summer weekend in October, I drove out to our camper to attend the Fall Festival and work on the cards I needed for the next weekend. Before I left the city, I assembled the materials I thought I would need. I packed card stock, watercolor paints, brushes, colored pencils, colored markers and a few books to search for a quote for the front of the cards.

Saturday morning, I went for my normal three-mile walk. I thought about the cards. I didn't know what design I was going to use; I didn't know what the cards were going to say. During the walk a thought came into my head: "Lord, as long as you are with me, I am not alone." The more I thought about it, the more I liked it. I had my quote, now all I needed was the design. Many activities were scheduled for Fall Festival, but when I had free time, I returned to the task at hand. The envelopes determined the size of the cards but I had to decide on word placement and the medium that I would use for the picture. I decided I would write an individual note on the inside during the next weekend after I met the women.

I quickly discovered that markers and water color paints bled through the paper. I could use a marker for the words but it would never do for the picture. I finally settled on colored pencils … dark clouds with the sun peeking out, birds and flowers or plants. I had twenty-four cards to make. I wanted each card to be different, not only for the participant but to exercise my own creativity.

On Sunday fewer activities were planned, ending with a pumpkin hunt at 1:00. I assembled my material on the picnic table outside and went to work. Making the cards was a slow process. Printing the letters in pencil, then going over them with a marker, then adding the design. I decided to finish the front of each card before going on to the next. By 1:30, I was seriously thinking of the pumpkin hunt. I needed a break. I put away my supplies and rode my scooter to the area of the hunt to see if there were any pumpkins left.

On the way I passed the campsite of an older gentleman, a permanent resident of the campground, who I hadn't seen that year. A man wearing bib coveralls and an engineer's hat was raking leaves. I turned around to talk to him. "How is Papa Joe?" I asked, "I haven't seen him."

"I'm Joe," the man replied. He had lost weight and grown a mustache. I hadn't recognized him. Papa Joe told me his story. One morning in the spring, Joe sat at his table drinking a cup of coffee at 7:00 A.M. He was very surprised when he couldn't lift the cup. Just then his phone rang. His daughter who never called that early was on the phone, checking on her father. When she heard his slurred speech, she phoned for emergency assistance. Joe was taken to the hospital, then a nursing home were he recovered from a stroke. This was his first weekend back at the campground. After we talked for a while, I left to search for a pumpkin. I was in luck; they had a large supply of pumpkins that year and I found one that was almost too big to carry on my scooter. Going slowly, my pumpkin and I made it back safely to our camper.

I brought out the material for the cards, sat down at the picnic table and picked up where I left off. It was a beautiful day. As I worked a gentle breeze blew. A twig fell off the tree and landed near my hand on the picnic table. I worked on the cards. In the process, I took out most of the 24 colored pencils from the case. The breeze picked up, I watched in amazement as the pencils rolled off the table, one after another, like little soldiers marching. I picked them up and went back to work. I made a few comments to the breeze and anyone else who happened to be listening … "It's a beautiful day! I want to finish the cards!"

A swarm of black bugs attacked me. I went inside, got insect repellent and sprayed myself. I was becoming frustrated. "I have my pumpkin, what else am I supposed to do?" I asked the breeze. I continued to work on the cards.

A small branch fell off the tree, hitting me on the head. I gave up. I put away the cards, markers, pencils. I locked the camper and went to visit friends who were heading south for the winter. I wanted to tell them that I had seen Papa Joe. I wanted to tell them about his early morning phone call from his daughter.

In 1999, I attended my first storytelling guild meeting. I decided to go to the next guild meeting and tell a story. I chose the story of the Fall Festival weekend. To refresh my memory, I reread the story I wrote. That is when I added this post-script—It has taken me three years to realize that I was given a message: "Put your work down, you have stories to tell."

PIPE DREAM

(I had begun the task of looking for a publisher for my memoir. Each week, I poured over the listings in the Writers Market, looking for companies that might publish my book. So far, I had received numerous rejections. I couldn't believe it when I opened the letter expecting a rejection; instead, it invited me to send in my manuscript. I mailed it off immediately. And now it was back. The letter accompanying the book suggested that the work needed editing. It referred me to a book doctor. The following thought ramble, a letter to my friend Rosie, was written the day after the book was returned, the day I phoned the book doctor.)

The time at the tone is 6:15 AM. Actually it is 6:45. I have been up for over a half-hour already. I can't tell my friends in high places that I don't need to be up, the book is at the publisher; there is nothing I can do. Because it isn't true anymore, but even when it was, they didn't listen to me anyway and the itch started.

I don't know how much of this letter I will send to you. At least this morning my computer is behaving. The last letter I wrote, the alarm started sounding. I didn't know the computer had an alarm; I didn't turn it on and had no idea how to shut it off. I turned off the computer a couple of times. First one thing went wrong, then another, the keys stuck, the keys wouldn't work, mischief was afoot. I thought of getting holy water, but I blessed the computer with my bare hand and the nonsense stopped.

I worry about me sometimes. It sounds as if I'm getting weird or paranoid. So many unexplained things have happened since my father passed over. Did I get a concussion when I was hit on the head by a picture of the Sacred Heart when I was fixing the hatch on the roof? But that wouldn't explain when I was caught—naked, in the shower with a head full of soap when the shower nozzle came off in my hand the day of Aunt Connie's funeral, the anniversary of my father's death. I couldn't turn off the water, or turn down the temperature. There was no one home to ask for help. I had to turn off the water in the basement, and use left over water from making tea to rinse the soap from my head.

I know that I am a determined child but I don't think that I have to be hit on the head or washed away before I listen, but then again, maybe I only respond to forceful attempts to get my attention. THAT IS NOT A COMFORTING THOUGHT.

I have found that it helps me to sort out my thinking, rambling away at the keyboard. Thanks for listening.

During the Mission I attended this week, the priest spoke of two forces—good and evil, light and dark. I believe that both are very busy helping me. I don't mind the light force, except when I'm hit on the head, but the dark one can leave, NOW!

I understand fully the shadows, as a writer friend puts it—the dark room that is hidden in your house, all of a sudden you open the door and fall in. Then because it is so dark, you can't find your way back out again. Or, this thought came to me this morning, you are walking and all of a sudden, the ground falls out from under you like in one of the famous sinkholes.

I am trying desperately to stay out of the shadows, not open the door to the dark room, not fall into the sinkhole.

While the book was at the publisher, I was having a marvelous time spending money—new carpeting for the floor, a new comforter for our bed, maybe paint and new curtains too. Lunch out somewhere … a play … a vacation. I knew they were going to publish it. It is a good thing I was only spending that money in my mind.

The book came back in yesterday's mail. The accompanying letter indicated that the subject had value, but that the work needed to be edited. They recommended a book doctor. The mail arrived too late to make any phone calls.

Our church is holding a Mission for Lent. Last night at the Mission, my prayer was: "God, please tell me what to do. Direct me please!" (My brain is always so busy that voices don't get through. Usually I don't dream at night, or remember the dream if I do. So I can't get messages through my dreams. Maybe that's why I get hit on the head. I would rather NOT be hit on the head.)

This morning, I went to church. I was going to talk to our crossing guard but she wasn't at church. Father Dennis celebrated the Mass. He started with the song: <u>There is a Balm in Gilead</u>

> There is a balm in Gilead, to make the wounded whole; there is a balm in Gilead, to heal the sin sick soul. Sometimes I feel discouraged and think my work's in vain, But then the Holy Spirit, Revives my soul again.

After Mass, I sat at McDonald's having a cup of coffee. Instead of the things I wanted to eat to sooth my spirit: chocolate, French fries, Big Mac, ice cream sundae—fat, cholesterol. On top of that, I am trying to do meatless Wednesday's for Lent. Writing down my thoughts: "What am I supposed to do? Have I received instructions and just don't want to listen? I can't talk to anyone I depend on! I would like to talk to someone. Tom said we could use our income tax money to pay for the book. Should I wait for the two publishers that are still out or make a phone call? Which editor—the one recommended by the publisher or the one recommended to me in Creative Writing?"

I feel like an octopus or a hunter. All my senses are alive looking for directions. I am a detective with my magnifying glass out looking under rocks for clues; I am a scientist, dissecting bits and pieces looking for answers. I am not smart enough to get the answer, find the clues.

How nice it was to return home, driving through the worsening snow, to see the mailman had already come. And there was a package from you. It made my day. I decided that I would open it after I made my phone call or calls.

Before I made my calls, I loaded up my phonograph with records. The records had been slowing down, then they just gave up and the turntable died.

The book doctor from the firm recommended by the publisher returned my call. He was very brisk, time is money attitude. I was on the phone with him for maybe ten minutes, probably less. He asked if I wrote a novel or non-fiction. I responded non-fiction. He didn't inquire into the subject but asked how many words. I mentioned the word count and the number of pages. He told me that publishers count 250 words to the page. He quickly ran down the list of his fees, he charges by the page. I won't bore you with the details. A person just cancelled a manuscript he was expecting. If I could get mine to him immediately, he would discount his prices. I told him I would have to think about it. I wasn't impressed.

Then I called the person recommended by my friend in Creative Writing. What a nice change. We were on the phone for more than 30 minutes. I won't bore you with the details but I decided to ask her to edit my book. It seemed that she would keep my voice, honor the subject. I called the publishing company to see if I could use her. I didn't receive an answer from them.

Then I opened the package from you. It contained lotion. I remembered the song I sang that morning and changed it to fit my day: "There was a balm from Rosie...."

TWO NOTES:

When I received the book back from the editor, I opened it at random. I wrote how my father found a spoon, bowl, cereal, sugar, and the milk for his breakfast. She changed it to he assembled the meal. Since my father had Alzheimer's disease, finding all the components for his breakfast was a huge undertaking. They were kept in different places. She lost the meaning of the sentence and that warned me to take her changes with a grain of salt. When I sent in the revised version, the publisher no longer wanted my book.

Years later, I learned that I had been taken in by a scam. Preying on dreams, the publisher and the book doctors took many aspiring writers to the cleaners. They had no plans to publish any of the books. Except for the book doctor's attitude, I would have been one of them.

BALLOONS

In my dream I was at a large gathering, giving a talk and I needed a way of demonstrating the topic. I decided to use the game where balloons are tied by string to the ankle of a person. The person who still has a balloon at the end of the game wins. As a person's balloon is broken, the person drops out of the game. As soon as the whistle blows, everyone scrambles to break another balloon, always trying to protect his or her own. The strings get in the way, people trip over the balloons.

When I thought about the dream, I reflected on how our grudges are like balloons. They trip us up when we are not expecting it. They stay out of our way so we forget them. Then something snags us, catches our attention, drags us back. The only way to be free is to cut the string.

The person who stands in a corner protecting their balloon loses as much as if they were taking a chance, participating in the game. They miss out on the laughter, the friendship and the interaction of others. By not wanting to take a chance on being hurt—on losing the game, they lose much more.

At Mass, a priest remarked that our hurt or grudge was like a hidden treasure, a brilliant ruby that needs to be discarded. Since nature doesn't like a vacant space, the emptiness, the void that the hurt occupied will be filled with the love of God, if we let it.

I realized that I had been given ammunition to use against the dragons, the "horns", the forces of evil that try to trip me; that try to drag me down into the dark, into the abyss. I have been given the love of God as armor, and a shield to protect me from harm. With this armor I'm never alone, I do not need to be afraid. I have been given the weapon of prayer to use when the battle is tough. The trick and it is a trick, because the conniver drags me down into the deep before I realize that I have slipped through the hole, is to recognize that I'm in the battle and use my armor and weapons to protect myself before I become wounded.

Possibly our negative thoughts help us to work out our disappointments and pain without hurting others. We just need to keep these thoughts under control, on a leash so that we remain the master, and not vise versa.

I was finished with this piece until I read this excerpt in *Called To Life, Called To Love* by Henri J.M. Nouwen, a Lenten reflection booklet I picked up at St. Catherine's in Orange Park, FL. "To forgive another person from the heart is an act of liberation. We set that person free from the negative bonds that exist between us … We also free ourselves from the burden of being the 'offended one.' As long as we do not forgive those who have wounded us, we carry them with us or, worse, pull them as a heavy load. The great temptation is to cling in our anger to our enemies and then define ourselves as being offended and wounded by them. Forgiveness, therefore, liberates not only the other but also ourselves … What are the grudges you are clinging to?"

I had an immense treasure, a raging, fiery ruby that I often pulled out of its box to examine. It was very sharp. As I looked at it, I would gently rub its point across my skin to see if it still hurt. Finding out that it did, I would carefully pack it away again until the next time. I always left a string attached to it so that it wouldn't get lost. That string would trip me up when I least expected it. A song on the radio, a passage in a book, or a movie would yank on the string so that it cut deeply into my skin. I couldn't free myself, I couldn't cut its string, or I didn't want to. I finally succeeded when I used a thought from Brenda Ueland in *If You Want To Write."* You will never know what your husband looks like unless you try to draw him, and you will never understand him unless you try to write his story." I combined her advice with prayer and looked at the ruby from a different perspective. As I looked at it from the shoes of another, the ruby lost its fire. I was able to cut the string that had shadowed me for so long.

ROSES WITH THE MORNING PAPER

My last day of work at a job that was hazardous to my health was on a Thursday. Since I am a practicing Catholic, the next morning found me at church saying "thank you" for my freedom. Not only was it the first Friday of March, it was the first Friday of Lent. I wondered what I was going to give up for Lent when I realized I had given up money. Free falling, I was depending on God to provide. I continue to go to Mass on Fridays, saying "thank you", for allowing me to be a free spirit.

The Feast day of the Sacred Heart Of Jesus fell on Friday, June 6, 1997. I planned to go to the 11:30 Mass at St. Peter's in Chicago's Loop. A special Mass was planned to celebrate the feast day, complete with trumpets, flutes, organ and choir. Since it was early and I had plenty of time, I lingered over my coffee, turning on the radio to catch the weather. Moving slowly, I didn't even bring in our morning paper. I was surprised when I heard the announcer warn of late morning thunderstorms. Rain had not been predicted for the day. I didn't want to be caught in the canyons of downtown when the wind whipped the rain. Too many times, my umbrella had been turned inside out as I fought both the wind and the rain. I decided to go to Mass at our neighborhood church instead. It wouldn't be a special Mass, no horns or choir but we would sing and the stained glass window over the altar honored the Sacred Heart.

Except, it was already eight o'clock and Mass started at eight thirty. I wasn't even dressed.

Moving quickly, I was ready to leave before fifteen minutes had passed. I needed the rest of the time to walk to church if I didn't want to be late. Glancing at our newspaper lying on the front porch, I was very surprised to see a rose lying next to it. I had planned to leave the paper on the porch until I returned but I wasn't going to leave a rose lying there. Grabbing both the paper and the rose, I retreated into the house. I didn't have time to admire the rose or cut its stem. Grabbing a wine glass, I filled it with water, inserted the rose and left. Meanwhile the questions had started. Who left the rose? My youngest daughter was on a vacation in Florida and her boyfriend knew she was gone. The rose couldn't be for her. The rose had to be for me but who left it? My son was staying with his girlfriend. My husband went to work at 5:30, before the paper arrived. It couldn't be from him. Who left the rose?

I told everyone I met about the rose with the Morning Edition. By then, I even knew who had given it to me. I decided the rose had to be from my neighbor. I had given her a story to read and I thought the rose was her way of saying thank you. After all, a rose bush was in bloom on the corner. I was sure the rose was from there. She could have picked one after she walked her son to school.

The rose looked great when I returned home. I decided to leave well enough alone and didn't cut the stem.

When my husband phoned, I told him about my surprise and asked if he had left it. "I wish I had," he said.

Roses don't last for a long time. To remember the gift, I took the rose, the paper and my camera out to the porch. Setting the scene, I took a few pictures to capture the moment. Then I put the rose back in the water in the wine glass.

Around noon, I saw my neighbor. "Thank you for the rose," I called to her. She looked at me as if I was nuts. I realized she wasn't the source of the gift and shared my experience of the morning. She had no idea who gave it to me.

Back to square one. I decided to try to figure out where the rose was cut from the bush. Taking the rose in my hand, I headed for the door. It was then I realized why the rose still looked so beautiful. It was silk. That is why it didn't wilt. I poured out the water but kept the rose in the wine glass.

I kept asking those I knew if they had given me the rose. Even made phone calls to a few friends. Nobody had. I never found out who did. I learned that St. Theresa, the Little Flower, sent a rose when your prayers were answered but I wasn't praying to her. I knew that the Blessed Virgin Mary's presence is announced with the scent of roses. Was it from her? The rose moved to a vase in the corner of my kitchen by the sink.

Ten years later, the rose still looks as beautiful as the day I received it. Rachel Naomi Remen wrote, "An unanswered question is a good traveling companion. It keeps your eyes on the road" And so it does.

WINGS

In 1998, the week of Christmas, I woke from a dream in which I was flying to Florida. Ready for takeoff, I couldn't leave as scheduled because I learned the CEO and the president wanted to fly with me. Muttering to myself, I walked over to change my plans. When I arrived at the control tower, the person at the desk said that I didn't need to come over personally; I could have used my radio. "I hadn't thought of it," I replied as I realized I was the pilot of the plane. As I turned from the desk with the new flight plans, I saw the CEO and the president walking in the wrong direction. The president was following a dog on a leash. I didn't recognize the dog.

"Good, I get new flight plans and there they go." I decided to return to my plane before getting the others. When I arrived at the spot where I left my plane, it wasn't there. I looked around but I didn't see it in the big, open hanger. I asked various workers if they had seen my plane. Each time I asked, I was directed to a different location. When I reached the new spot, the plane was gone. Back and forth I searched, from one end of the building to another without success. I got so frustrated I picked up the public address system and demanded, "Whoever has my plane, bring it back. It is too big to hide in a shoebox." My anger woke me, but as I woke, I saw two men on a tractor pulling a Blue Angel Thunderjet. They were complaining, "Looks like we goofed, I thought they were finished with this plane. Why don't they make up their minds!"

On Christmas Eve I received four eagle statues from Sue and Ivan. They represented different parts of flight—take off, soaring, hunting, and landing. Christmas Day brought more wings. I received a frosted plastic tree top angel holding a trumpet and three smaller angel ornaments of the same design from Bill. Sue gave me three angel icicle ornaments holding a flute, violin and harp.

I hadn't told my dream to my family. On Christmas morning after we opened presents, I shared the dream. Bill commented, "Looks like you have earned your wings."

When we moved into our house we bought our Christmas tree. Bill was the baby and Tom didn't want him crawling on the floor, putting needles into his mouth. Years passed, and now, the tree looked more real each year as the branches sag and bare spots appear. Once it is decked out with all of the lights and ornaments and garlands, it looks very real. There was always room for the new ornaments that are added each year. Bill referred to it as a Charlie Brown tree.

I usually put our tree up the first week of December. But I was late putting up our Christmas tree in 1999.

After the tree was up, and the lights were on, I asked Sue if she wanted to put on some of the ornaments. She did. Last year I had saved a box of special ornaments for her and Bill to put on but I had decorated the tree with the rest, using up much of the available space. I didn't want to do the same thing again. The tree looked very sad without any ornaments on it. I put the thirty sequin ornaments on the bottom that we made when we first bought our house. The sequins were not as bright as when they were new but they brought back memories as I placed the ones made by Tom and my father. I knew which ones were mine; they had beads along with the sequins. The tree didn't look as bare. Then I climbed the stepstool to hang the tiny glass ornaments on the top, some were lead and belonged to my grandmother—leaving the middle unadorned. The middle looked too bare. Then I remembered an ornament where Santa Clause raided the refrigerator, it had to be plugged into a light; I found it a place. I remembered Santa resting in a reclining chair with a deer at his feet. He required a large space and a perfect spot was found. I decided to put up my angels also.

I started with the six new angels I received last year, 3 from Sue and 3 from Bill plus the treetop angel. Next I tried to put up the older 6 smaller angels I bought when I was in high school. Less than two inches tall, dressed in pastel gowns, they each held a tiny, different musical instrument. They always occupied the top of the tree.

That is when the trouble began. The older angels didn't want to stay on the tree, they kept dropping to the floor or the hooks came off. If everything else worked, they seemed to be perfect in a spot that was already occupied. Dueling angels. I finally became frustrated and discussed with anyone who would listen, dog, cat, spirit, dust—I was the only one home—"This fighting is silly. It has to stop. NOW! Christmas is a time of peace. No one is any better than the other one." ETC! The date of this activity was Dec 17.

Taking down the tree, I began to remove the older angels, leaving the new ones on just a little longer. The dueling began all over again. Angels that I didn't touch fell from the tree. A bit of glue fixed most of the damage.

(My oldest daughter, Kathy, told me that the angels weren't fighting or feuding, they were being persnickety. They wanted me to recognize the stature of the older angels and give them first pick of the choice places.)

I've learned my lesson. Each year my tiny older angels are the first to take their spot on the top of the tree and the last to be removed. I no longer credit my father for all the "HELP" I receive. I finally realized that my mother and brother have been assisting me for a long time. They were skilled; they did it without attracting my attention. After all, who better than a mother to know that your daughter is independent and stubborn and needs guidance?

THE STORYTELLER

I woke from the dream, the images fresh in my mind. In my youth, I looked like a typical Swedish girl—fair skinned, blonde hair, blue eyes. The hair is becoming more frosted as I age and I wear it shorter now, but the eyes and skin have remained the same.

In my dream I brushed my long black hair, blue eyes staring back from the mirror out of a pecan colored face. I looked down at my hands and was amazed as the pecan skin color raced up my arms. The girl in the mirror looked like a Native American Indian. And I woke.

Walking to church, I pondered the meaning of my dream. A couple of weeks before, I attended an oral presentation of a creative writing class where the students read their stories. When I was enrolled in the class, I read some of my own stories. I was no longer in the class but I continued to attend the end of semester readings.

This presentation was different. One of the students told a story instead of reading. I was intrigued and asked the woman a few questions. I learned a story telling guild met on the third Wednesday of the month at the homes of the members. During the evening storytellers gathered to practice their craft. I also learned that the doors were open to guests.

At the beginning of the year, I was at Chicago's Art Institute on a day when Shanta, a storyteller, was a featured guest. I hadn't known that a special event was being held. At the right place, at the right time—I waited in line, found a seat, and listened to stories. Time passed too quickly.

The next month, I discovered that The Field Museum was hosting an International storytelling event. Interested—I attended.

Now I was presented with the opportunity to investigate a story telling guild. But did I want to become a storyteller? That was the question. When my book was published I would need to speak in public but did I want to be a storyteller? And then I had the dream.

As I walked, I pondered the dark color racing up my arms in the dream. The black hair! Without trying, I realized that I had gradually become a storyteller. Before my father passed, I often told the story of my neighbor's bout with the wasp. When the occasion was right, I told the story of my rosary turning gold. After my father died, I added the story of Pap and The Pancake Turner to my list of stories.

CATHEDRALS— SOUTH DAKOTA

Note: Our first trip in many years took us to the Black Hills in South Dakota. We invited our youngest daughter, Sue, to go with us and asked our son and his wife to watch our aging dog. I was still trying to get our book published. When we returned from our trip, I wrote a 21-page journal of our experience, which I shared, with our children. Finding the journal when I was working on this book, I tried to cut the fluff but keep the journey. Of course, Dad is my husband Tom)

Saturday as I finished the last minute details preparing for our trip, I was pleased—I was ahead of schedule. I looked at the hip pouch I was using for a purse and decided that I could lighten it. Then I noticed that my pouch was beginning to rip. I decided to replace it for the trip from the stash I had in the linen closet. As I transferred the items from one pouch to another, I decided to leave everything that wasn't essential at home. The last thing I lightened was my change purse. As I removed the extra paper from my change purse I realized that I didn't remember seeing my driver's license. My heart sank! My driver's license was missing! Where could it be? I tried to remember the last place I had used it. Then I remembered … on Thursday, downtown at Filene's Basement when I wrote a check. Dad suggested that I call them before I searched further. Sure enough! They had my driver's license in their safe. I was very happy to get my driver's license back and glad that I discovered that it was missing before we left for our trip. I knew I would need it for identification for writing checks on the trip if not for driving. On the way back from downtown, Dad told me that he and Sue would do all the driving so I could relax and enjoy the scenery.

I had hoped to leave for Bill and Michelle's house at noon but losing my driver's license delayed us. We managed to leave around 1:00. We had our own convey as Dad and Sue both drove their cars to Bill's. I planned to leave my car at their house with Cuyler (our dog). Sue planned to drive her car to the camper and leave it there until we returned.

Our journey to Rapid City, South Dakota began on June 20, 1999, Father's Day. After 7:30 Mass at Our Lady Of Perpetual Help in Sublette, we left the camper around 9:00 A.M,

The Thursday before we left for South Dakota, I went to Jewel to buy supplies for the trip. Only one checkout was open when I finished shopping. The woman in line ahead of me had two small boys contained in her shopping basket. One sat with his dinosaurs in the seat where children sit. The other sat in the bottom of the basket with his blanket. The woman's groceries were stored on the shelf below.

The mother asked if I wanted to go ahead of her but I declined. I was having too much fun watching the boys. The person bagging the groceries apologized for not putting the groceries in the cart. There was nowhere to put them. The mother replied, "That's all right, I try to keep the boys in the cart as long as I can." I could tell from the tone of her voice that her boys were full of mischief. The woman behind me asked if the boys were twins. The mother replied that they weren't twins. They were thirteen months apart but it was almost like having twins. Then she told us her story. She and her husband had an only child, a fifteen-year-old son when they went on vacation. Nine months later they were gifted with another son. Thirteen months later. They had their third.

Thursday evening I told Dad the mother's story. I also said that the only thing I wanted to give birth to from our vacation was a book.

Monday morning, in Jackson, MN, Promise joined our family. (Promise is a stuffed doll that is toddler size. She hides her face in her hands.) Sue was still sleeping when we stood the doll next to the wall where Sue would see her when she opened her eyes.

"Oh dear! ... I wasn't expecting to see a little child," Sue exclaimed when she saw Promise standing there.

We stopped at Al's Oasis for lunch. Along with a souvenir shop, the Oasis had a large grocery store attached—Mueller's General Store since 1919, the sign proclaimed. Since we had already drank half of the water I had brought with us, I bought a six-pack of water—I was glad that I did. The drive ahead became very hot. We finished the last of the water that I had brought from home and half of the water that I bought at Mueller's before we arrived in Rapid City. The landscape after we crossed the Missouri became desolate, rolling grass covered hills, with hardly a tree to be seen. Farms and houses were miles from each other. Every once and a while a hill was covered with yellow sweet clover, which is considered a trash plant, good for nothing in that part of the country, neither cows or horses will eat it. Bee hives where located near some of those yellow hills. The wind blew with a gale force, bending anything that had the courage to grow. The theme of the drive was repeated and repeated when I heard the same song over and over again on the radio, The Color Of The Wind, from Pocahontas. A woman at a rest stop summed up the day when she said, "Windy isn't it! I haven't combed my hair all day."

We saw many signs for Wall Drugs. Quite a few advertised free ice water. Some of the gas stations advertised shaded fill-ups. As the hot miles flew by, we could understand how both would be welcome. The desolate landscape stretched as far as the eye could see. Not a cloud shaded the sky.

As we neared the Black Hills, the landscape changed again, it became greener. The Black Hills rose in the distance. The skies clouded. The temperature dropped a few degrees making the drive bearable. We were ready for a cool hotel room.

As I walked across the parking lot to get more stuff from the car, my sandal broke. Although I had ridden barefoot, I lived in my sandals whenever we had to get out of the car during the drive.

After dinner Monday night, we dropped Dad off at the hotel and followed the clerk's instructions to get to Wal-Mart. We made a right hand turn out of the parking lot, drove 1 block down the hill, and I saw a church steeple. As Sue made a left turn onto Fifth Ave., I looked at the name of the church. A sign proudly proclaimed Our Lady Of Perpetual Help Cathedral and listed the times of the daily masses. I didn't know what to say. When we are at the camper, we attend Our Lady Of Perpetual Help church.

First we found Shop Ko where with Sue's help, I found a pair of sandals for $5. We also bought more water: 2 six packs at $1.99 each. I had paid $3.19 at Al's Oasis for one 6-pack. We picked up some things that I forgotten to pack along with the Pocahontas CD.

We soon discovered that the sun rises earlier in the Black Hills and also sets later in the day, lengthening the daylight by about an hour.

Tuesday morning I was awake bright and early, 5:30 A.M. Mountain Time. Dad had gotten up to go to the bathroom but his snoring soon confirmed that he had been able to fall back to sleep. Sue put a pillow over her head and was still, I couldn't go back to sleep.

After I finished my exercises, I didn't know what to do with myself. Before I left the room, I left a note for my family saying that I went to Mass.

Time passed slowly. Leaving the hotel, the air felt cool. I decided to get my jacket from the car. I was very surprised when our car wasn't where we had left it. I saw an empty space. Maybe I was mistaken where we had parked it but after a quick glance around the parking lot I didn't see our car. I had an empty feeling, and didn't know what to do. I returned to the hotel and told the desk clerk that our car was missing. When I described our car to her, she said she remembered it. Her's was the red car parked next to it. It was there at 11:00 P.M. when her shift began. "Were the doors locked?" she asked. She reached for the phone to call our room but I didn't want Dad and Sue to be woken hearing that our car was stolen. I went back to our room and was very surprised to see that not only was our bed empty, the bathroom was empty too.

I was relieved. I figured that wherever my husband was, his car was with him. I returned to the front desk and told the clerk that my husband was also missing.

Leaving the hotel, I scanned the nearby gas station and saw our car sitting by a pump. I found Dad inside the gas station, paying for his purchases. When I told him about the scare that he had given me, he said that he looked for me in the breakfast area but didn't see me. Since I hadn't put down any time on my note, he figured I had gone to church. I asked him to let the desk clerk know that he had our car and left for Mass.

The Cathedral Of Our Lady Of Perpetual Help is impressive. As I approached the side door, I noticed a granite or marble etching of a guardian angel protecting a little girl and a little boy, who stood with his back to me, hiding his face in his hands. These words were inscribed next to the figures:

Child of God
Live this day,
As if it were your first day,

As if it were
Your last day,

As if it were
Your only
Day.

When I entered the cathedral, I heard voices saying the rosary. I didn't want to be late for Mass and headed for the room that held the voices. They were in a beautiful chapel. The many titles of Our Lady were inscribed on the windows.

I picked up their church bulletin: <u>The Voice of the Cathedral</u>. The reflections for Father's Day, the Twelfth Sunday in Ordinary Time contained a sketch of a cross with these words: "Jesus said to them DO NOT BE AFRAID." The writer added: "Even when raw fear for ourselves or our loved ones makes our hair stand on end, God promises to be among us."

No matter where I wander the message is the same: "Be Not Afraid, I go before you, come follow me and I will give you peace." These words give me confidence to walk through the day and not worry about tomorrow. It is a relief to be able to say that, especially when it appears that the publishing of our story will become a reality and life, as I know it will change drastically. It has taken quite a while before I have been able to reach this point. To stop worrying about every molehill that popped up. To trust that I would be given what I needed when I needed it, but the journey has been worth it.

Since the weather report suggested that Tuesday would be the coolest day of the week, we decided to go to the Badland's.

Entering the badlands, a sign indicated a prairie dog town. Following the sign, we took the gravel, dirt road to the side. The road was very rough, I worried about the effect the gravel and ruts would have on our car.

Many places were provided to pull off the road and admire the view. The badlands are beautiful in their own way; I was surprised to see so many wild flowers and grasses. The song of birds was everywhere. The prairie dog village was worth the trip. They are amazing animals; Dad captured my voice on tape as I tried to convince an individual to come out of its den with its family.

I used at least two rolls of film in the badlands. Each overlook had its own special beauty and required at least two pictures to capture it. Sue and I weren't very adventurous climbing the rocks until we reached the east end of the park where we became braver.

I saw and heard a meadowlark singing on a bush. The song of the meadowlark followed us through the Badlands. At one stop, I caught a flash of blue and orange on the wing, a blue bird flew past. A black bird with white streaks caught my eye at a guided hiking trail and for the first time I met a black-billed magpie.

The sky darkened when we reached Wall Drugs. Dad forgot to put down the sunroof and wasn't happy when his key wouldn't unlock the driver's door. The driver's door wouldn't unlock with my key either or with the button on the passenger door. The driver's door lock was jammed. Dad couldn't free it. I finally suggested that I would see if I could buy some WD 40 or graphite to free the lock. They didn't have either at the drug store, which was supposed to have everything. I was referred to Ace Hardware at the edge of town. Walking back to the car from Ace, I found a rock that reminded me of the stone I saw in the Badlands and picked it up. The graphite worked momentarily, allowing the door to open once but it soon jammed again. Dad finally gave up and we went for something to eat. The sky opened up and it poured. The rain let up when we left for the hour drive back to Rapid City.

On the way back to the hotel, I suggested that we look for a garage to fix his door in the morning. I didn't think it was safe for us to be traveling in a car where the driver's door wouldn't open. Sue heard a scrapping sound coming from the rear wheel. It might only be gravel from the prairie dog excursion but I figured we could have that checked at the same time.

Wednesday morning I woke very early again. As I did some exercises in the bathroom, Dad joined me. Since he was up, he decided to accompany me to Mass. We couldn't do anything about the car until eight o'clock at the earliest.

As I ate breakfast, Dad phoned Action Auto, the first name on our list. Al said he could repair our door in an hour; we wouldn't need to rent a car.

There was nothing to do in the area where Action Auto was located. We wandered through a small drug store, investigated what they termed the "mall"—a barbershop, pet store, beauty shop, floral shop, grocery store, and casino. On the way to Action Auto, the rear brakes on Dad's car had locked and when the car door was fixed, Dad asked Al to look at the rear wheels. Al found that a spring on the wheel cylinder had broken causing the rubbing sound Sue heard. The wheel cylinder would have come apart before much more time passed. The parts delivery van brought the wrong cylinder and had to return for another one. As we waited, I watched a woman try to unlock the door to the building in front of the garage. When she wasn't successful, I gave her the graphite we had in our car. It freed her lock. There was a bead store in front of the garage, which I thought she owned. I was mistaken. The bead store wouldn't open until 11:00 A.M.

We were still waiting for our car when the bead store opened. I knew I would have a good time before I entered the store and I was right. I let my eyes wander around the small store when I entered. Most of the items reflected Native American culture. The store contained more than just beads. I wandered to a rack that held T-shirts where a bright peach shirt made me laugh. A cat wearing a bird rescue unit tank top dangled from a branch next to a yellow bird. The writing advised "Hang in there, baby!" I didn't know if the advice was for the cat or the bird. Not content, I kept going through the shirts and discovered a design that was unique. The artist Tatansa Wostal Maw's work was exclusive to the bead shop. I was told I wouldn't see it anywhere else in the Black Hills. The Black Hills appeared in the background on the shirt, in front of which was a tree and a butterfly. Lightning cracked from the sky. The silhouette of a buffalo skull rose up to the heavens in a star studded sky. The shape of a pyramid appeared in the lower part of the buffalo's skull. The profile of a howling wolf overlaid one of the buffalo's horns while a profile of an eagle balanced the other. The design was definitely unique. I had no choice! I had to buy those shirts. Then I found a bead book that interested me. Next I decided to buy some beads so I would have something to do in the hotel room. The owner, Deanna, has a daughter who lives in Forrest Park, IL, a southern suburb of Chicago. Time passed quickly as we chatted.

When I left the store, I was happy to learn that the car was fixed. The cost was a little more than one hundred dollars. Not bad! As Dad settled the bill, I realized that I needed an assortment of colored beads and returned to the store.

We stopped for lunch at Colonial House before going to Custer State Park. We drove up Needles highway and where impressed by granite spires, especially one section named "Cathedral Spires". I knew that I didn't have enough film for our trip. Everywhere we looked a photo opportunity beckoned, I was very glad that we had been directed to Action Garage as the narrow road rose … turned … dipped … and turned … following snakes. Many tunnels allowed the passage of only one car at a time.

We passed mountain climbers preparing to scale the rocks. We took the animal loop in the park but by the time we arrived, the buffalo herd had moved to Iron Mountain road. We saw a lone bull buffalo feeding by itself in the trees, a mule deer, a white tailed deer and some pronghorn antelopes. The country was beautiful. Many movies were filmed at that location including Dances with Wolves and the television series Gunsmoke.

Next we drove to Mount Rushmore where we viewed the evening lighting ceremony. After the flag was raised, a movie was shown that explained the reasons that the sculptor picked the four presidents depicted on the monument: George Washington was father of our country, Thomas Jefferson was instrumental in the Declaration Of Independence, Abraham Lincoln continued the work of establishing freedom for all and Theodore Roosevelt, who founded the first national park in Yellowstone, was instrumental in preserving our country.

Thursday morning, Dad joined me at morning Mass. As we left the Cathedral, the shape of the clouds reminded me of an angel flying with outstretched arms over our heads.

The brochure for the wild mustang ranch didn't have a map. We drove through town looking for signs without success. Then we saw a tourist information building.

Arriving at the ranch, Joe, a volunteer from Mississippi offered to take us on an unscheduled tour if more people came. Soon two other cars joined us for a special bus guided tour. The ranch is over 11,000 acres and more than 300 horse run free. Most were in the backcountry but some are pastured so that the tourists can see the horses. The off spring of the pastured horses are sold to support the ranch.

The film Crazy Horse was filmed on the ranch. The film company built a town for the film and left it for the ranch's use. We saw circles of grass growing in front of some teepees that National Geographic has determined to be 1200 years old. They belonged to the Anasasie Indians.

The Sioux had just finished holding a sun dance a few days before we toured. The center tree and squaw shelter was still standing, as was the sweat lodge.

We drove into the enclosure that held the pastured mustangs and heard the story of Frosty. She is a white mare that is spirited and full of mischief. Her ears are clipped from frostbite. She jumps the fences to go visit her friends and when Wells Fargo was there recently to film a commercial, Frosty led the horses in a different direction every time they had them encircled to move them to a different pasture. I knew that I had received the name for the painting of the white horse that I planned to do.

Joe told us he had spotted a golden eagle playing with the prairie dogs that morning. We were fortunate to see the same eagle buzzing the prairie dogs when we passed.

As Joe turned a bend in the grass, we were delighted and surprised when we came upon a band of mustangs on the move. Joe exclaimed, "You don't see that every day. See how skittish they are." Try as I might. The way the bus was bouncing I couldn't get a picture of them. There were more than twenty. Some accompanied by foals.

On the way back, we stopped at the Mammoth site. They have discovered the remains of more than 21 animals and are still working to uncover more of the bones buried there.

Leaving the Mammoth site, we drove route #385 through Wind Cave National Park on the way to Custer National Park. We took Iron Mountain road and quickly came to a stop as the buffalo herd moved down the center of the road. Cows and their calves passed on both sides of our car, snorting to each other. After more than a hundred animals walked passed our car, we started up again only to be stopped by a herd of wild donkeys who think that the main purpose of people traveling on that road is to feed them. They poke their noses into the cars, begging for food. They are tame enough to pet, which we did. We also fed them carrots.

I was at 7:00 A.M. Mass on Friday morning, June 25th, the anniversary of my mother's birth. The priest began the Mass with sad news, a fellow priest had been admitted to the hospital the preceding day with pneumonia and he was in intensive care, not responding to medication. His homily that morning began, "God has a plan. When we are suffering or when we watch others suffer, it is important for us to remember that God has a plan. Not only for physical healing but also for spiritual healing. Often we need to pray to find the root of the problem. You can bring others to Jesus for healing. If we bring our imagination to Him, He will help us to pray."

When we neared the town of Sturgis, the location of the huge Harley Davidson rally in August, I suggested we stop so Dad could see what the town looked like. Many streets where closed as the town prepared for the coming of the bikers. As we drove through the town, I noticed a sign pointing to Bear Butt state park and suggested that we check it out. The area was flat and mostly grasslands, no trees. I was curious what a state park would look like in that area. We turned a bend in the road and saw a high mountain off in the distance, which turned out to be Bear Butt State Park. At the park house, which also housed an Indian museum, we watched a film in which we discovered that Bear Butt was a volcano that never exploded. It is a sacred mountain to the Indians. The Oglala Chief Frank Fools Crow regularly came to the mountain to receive spiritual guidance and direction. The tradition of the Sioux said that four sacred feathers were received on the mountain, the four laws that governed the people. (I forgot to write down the laws but they were similar to the first four laws of the Ten Commandments.)

A park ranger, a schoolteacher from Sturgis, told us many things about the area, including the fact that South Dakota ranks lowest for teachers salaries. He has noticed recently that Native American children are beginning to show pride in their heritage and raise their hands when he asks if any are Indian.

The ranger said that the glacier didn't cross the Missouri river. The land to the West never received the rich soil. The land was only good for ranching.

He also told us that we were visiting at a very sacred time for the Indians. It was the time of the summer solstice. Many were on the mountain fasting and praying, hanging prayer flags. We should respect their traditions if we walked on the mountain and not disturb the Indians.

The mountain was recovering from a forest fire that destroyed most of the trees in 1996. Wild flowers were abundant. We drove up to the parking lot that was located a long hike from the top of the mountain. A park ranger sat in a shaded three-sided hut, by the entrance to the path. I'm sure his job was to inform visitors of the spirituality of the place and ask them to respect the Indian's beliefs.

Dad stopped just inside the trail, in an area that had benches and was shaded. Sue and I decided to walk up the mountain. I knew I wouldn't go all the way to the top. The day was too hot and I didn't have the right shoes for hiking. We passed an older Indian woman sitting off the path making prayer flags, a young girl played near her. I passed an Indian brave wearing a headset, carrying bundles of sage that he had gathered on the mountain.

I offered a prayer for guidance for us on our journey. Then I said a prayer for peace, within the individual … the family … the city or town … the state, nation, country and world. A flock of goldfinch flew past when I finished. I looked at the many prayer flags hanging from the trees in various colors: red, black, many were grey. Tobacco bundles hung from some trees, as did a pair of glasses festooned with prayer ties. Purple cornflowers were in bloom. Primrose grew next to the trail as well as other flowers that I recognized but couldn't name.

I passed two older white women with walking sticks descending the mountain trail. The older Indian woman passed me, using a walking stick to help her climb. The child tagged along behind, "I'm already tired!" She complained. "You'll make it," I encouraged her. "She did last year," the older woman said.

I had climbed a little higher than Sue on the path. Rejoining Sue, we descended the mountain trail and rested in the shade of the bench area. I offered a prayer for the Indian people, for help in fighting the addictions that held so many prisoner. A goldfinch landed on a branch nearby. I hated to leave, it was such a peaceful place but we had places to go and people to see,

I had thought that I spotted a bald eagle flying overhead as we turned onto the road leading to Bear Butt and felt that we had been spirit directed to the mountain.

Our next stop was Deadwood, which was HOT. Street parking was next to impossible to find. The town has several parking lots and runs a trolley that only costs .50 a ride which stops at all the casinos and hotels and motels in and near town. We found a spot to park the car and rode the trolley. We stopped in a few casino's, ate an ice cream cone, watched a reenactment of the shooting of Wild Bill Hickcock in the #10 saloon and rode the trolley back to our car to drive to a gold mine. Then Sue and I visited the cemetery on a high hill above town while

Dad rested in the shade of a tree. Wild Bill Hickcock rested next to Calamity Jane. I was surprised to learn that he was born in Troy Grove, IL, a little town south of Mendota, near where we camp.

The news at church the next morning wasn't good. Father Joe, who had just been admitted to the hospital on Thursday, was near death.

I found the morning readings to be thought provoking. First: Sarah is promised a son this time next year, Genesis 18:1–15. Then in Matthew 8: 5–17, "The Lord chooses us, he calls us to serve." Instead of a homily, the priest led the assembly in prayers for the peaceful passing of his friend.

Dad needed some down time. Sue and I wandered to Rapid City's Dinosaur park where we learned that Auatotitan, a duck-billed dinosaur lived in South Dakota during the late Cretaceous age, 65 million years ago. Somehow I never pictured dinosaurs in the United States, I always thought of them as European and African creatures.

We went to the chapel on the hill, a wooden church built as a replica of the wooden Lutheran churches in Norway. Six weddings were being held at the chapel that day. We arrived between two. The bride in the first wedding appeared to be older, dressed in a long white gown and veil. We learned that they were celebrating their twenty-fifth anniversary.

Dad had a dream the night before in which he went through a tunnel. He slid down a slide and dropped my camera where it broke into many pieces. Storms were forecast for the day. I wasn't sure that we should be wandering through the narrow, twisting, turning Black Hills roads of Custer State Park in a storm so we went to the museum—The Journey, in Rapid City. The museum chronicled the lives of the Indians, prospectors and settlers as South Dakota was settled. Wands were provided through which we could hear the voices of the Indians and settlers. The museum brought the history of the country to life.

It was still early when we finished the tour of the museum. We ate lunch at the Colonial House, then since the weather appeared to be clearing, we headed for Custer State Park. We stopped at Sylvan Lake instead of taking the Needles highway. The sign of a hiking trail pointed to Harney Peak, 3 miles away. Although my leg wasn't too swollen, I knew it wouldn't stand up to a six mile round trip hike. Instead we climbed on the rocks and watched the birds and the fish and a chipmunk. A man was fishing for rainbow trout which he released when he caught them.

The sky cleared, white clouds chased away the storm clouds. We decided to walk around the lake. Each time we climbed around a grouping of rocks, the scene changed. Many photo opportunities presented themselves. A sign gave this history of the area: "HILLS OF TIME ... The time worn Harney Peak, Needles and Cathedral Spires show their age and suggest to many that the Black Hills may be the oldest mountain range in the world. The Hills have a storehouse of geologic information which began hundreds of millions of years ago. They are comprised of (starting from the bottom) Schist Quartz, Granite, Deadwood sandstone, Winnipeg Shale, Paha Sapa limestone and Minnelusa Sandstone. The Black Hills rose 14,000 feet above sea level. Due to erosion, they rise 7,000 feet today."

On our trip around the lake, we met another couple heading the opposite way. The man told us that he had climbed the Harney Peak trail when he was younger. The trip took him all day. When he began to climb the mountain, he walked for a short time. Then rested for 15 minutes before repeating the process again. "I was in much better shape then," he said.

I was glad that we had decided not to take that trail.

As we arrived at the hotel, we noticed dark clouds roll in. The area was under a severe thunderstorm watch for many hours. As we returned from our last dip in the hot tub ... Sue's dip, my dangle ... (I had a leg ulcer) we saw a rainbow. But more dark clouds rolled in. The sky opened and hail pelted everything for over 5 minutes. We were glad that we were inside.

Monday morning we wanted to get an early start but I still had time to go to morning Mass. Except they didn't have one. Because of the passing of the priest, whoever was scheduled to say the Mass must have forgotten. We had a Communion service instead complete with readings and a homily that reflected on Abraham's courage to stand before God about the cities of Sodom and Gomorra. "What gave Abraham the courage to stand before God and challenge him? ... We are called to express our faith in action."

As Dad and I walked back to the hotel, I remarked that I often debated with God as Abraham did. "No wonder you get so much help," Dad replied, "You have to be persuaded." Somehow I felt that he had hit the nail squarely on the head.

As we neared the South Dakota border, I began working on my first pair of beaded earrings.

I finished two more pair of earrings on the trip, making a total of 6. The last pair I made as we entered Illinois, reminded me of our home state, white with turquoise—the white caps on the waves of Lake Michigan against the blue water and sky.

We arrived at the camper at 12:30. Sue and I were on the road again by 1:00. She was driving me to Bill & Michelle's house to get Cuyler. When we entered their house, we couldn't find the boy. Finally I spotted a note that said, "Houdini is in the garage." When Bill & Michelle came home from work they told me that no matter how they tried to barricade Cuyler in the kitchen, he escaped.

When I returned home on Wednesday, July 7, I received two pieces of sad news. There had been a message from my cousin, Bob, on our answering machine. Uncle Alvin passed over in a nursing home on June 21. The second piece of sad news, Brian, a young man from Montana discovered Beetles in our tree on 7/6. The tree would be cut down on 7/8.

Our elm tree had survived the Dutch elm disease that killed most of the Elm trees in our area in the 60's. It didn't survive the Asian beetle.

Winkler tree service arrived before 8:00 on Thursday morning to begin cutting down our tree. Commonwealth Edison stopped our electric service and the work of the day began. I had found a watch lying in some plants as I cleaned up the yard that morning. I felt it belonged to the fellow who found the beetles in our tree. I didn't think he needed to lose his watch just because our tree was losing its life, even though I knew it was an Indian custom. I asked the people from the tree company to return the watch to him. They had to remove our back fence to get the cherry picker into the yard. Even working from the bucket, Jose didn't drop the trunk until 4:00 P.M. Commonwealth Edison turned our electric back on soon after. At 8:00 P.M. they finally finished cutting out the tree's roots. The tree service workers had put in a very long, hot day. Our tree was 85 years old, 39" in diameter at chest height and had the distinction of having the largest root base in the city.

Friday night I went out to water the remaining flowers in the backyard. They had been uprooted when the tree was cut down and didn't look very healthy. I was sad, our yard looked barren and I missed our tree. I saw our neighbor to the south who was also grieving our tree. Lorna is an artist and has used our tree in many of her sketches. I mentioned that I knew that the souls of humans and animals passed over on their death, I wondered about trees. I had considered our tree my friend and I missed it. Lorna told me that she had an awake dream in which the trees appeared to her as women, reaching their branches (arms) out to give her a hug, or protect her from harm. Therefore Lorna felt that the spirit of the tree would pass over. I can like that, it makes me feel better anyway,

*   *   *   *

Tuesday July 13, author Frank Joseph, while speaking at Transitions bookstore about his new book *Synchronicities And You* recognized the mountain on my South Dakota T-shirt as Bear Butt. "It is the second most spiritual place in the world, right next to Pipestone, MN", he told us.

*   *   *   *

The next time we attended Mass at Our Lady of Perpetual Help in Sublette, I told the pastor, Fr. Hughes, how we attended Mass at the Cathedral of Our Lady Of Perpetual Help in Rapid City, SD. He remarked, "We follow our people every where."

ILLINOIS
STORYTELLING
FESTIVAL '99

Note: I planned to write a story about the Storytelling Festival for the book. Looking through my notes, I was very pleased to see I jotted a note to myself to see file: Festival '99. The original story is 8 pages long. Will I edit it or leave it as written? Good question, we will both soon know the answer. In the story you will see references to a cardinal, which was my Aunt Connie's favorite bird. She passed over in 1996, I always thought of her when I heard a cardinal sing. (I hope you enjoy reading the story as much as I did!)

Over 1,000 people braved the 90+ temperatures on Saturday to attend the Illinois Storytelling Festival in Spring Grove, IL.

When I arrived, I heard a cardinal sing and I knew it was going to be a good day. A cardinal had greeted me at the Storytelling Festival in Schaumburg in March and I had a marvelous time.

I had signed up to attend a workshop given by Peter Cook who is deaf. As I walked over to the workshop I realized that I didn't know sign language and asked myself what I was doing. I shouldn't have worried, arrangements had been made for those who didn't understand sign, a person interpreted the sign language into voice. Most of the participants KNEW and WERE FLUENT in sign. When I introduced myself, I mentioned that I was ignorant of the language.

After the workshop was over, I realized that it was a good thing that I hadn't talked myself out of attending. 1) I had a really good time. 2) I might be speaking to someone who doesn't know English and gestures will be helpful in getting my point across.

The stories were great, the storytellers very talented. I came home with many tapes and CD's along with books and permission to tell some of the stories I had heard.

I realized during the weekend that I have crossed a bridge since the first festival I attended last year. Last year I was just a member of the audience, enjoying the stories. This year I was still a member of the audience but I was also a storyteller who was learning from experts. So I paid more attention to their style of telling— gestures, facial expressions, movement. Of course, Peter Cook's workshop helped, it had set the scene.

As I left Sunday night, I heard a cardinal sing. How fitting, I thought, I had a GREAT TIME!

I sent the above e-mail to friends and family on Monday after the festival. It was a quick summary of an absolutely, marvelous time. But that is what it was, a summary. In order to do justice to the weekend ... I have to write a bit more about it. The following notes are from my notebook:

I parked my car in the last spot available next to the trees. The space was in sunshine but I was hoping that by evening it would be in shade and my car would be cooler. It was almost 9:00 AM. The workshops would soon be starting. As I walked over to St. Peter's church down a shady path, I heard a cardinal sing.

I passed people with bagels in their hands going in the opposite direction and confirmed that I was going the right way. Registration was held in the church basement where two other workshops were being held. But Peter's workshop was held in a mobile classroom in the opposite direction from the church.

As I hurried back towards the school, I realized that I had signed up for a deaf workshop. I didn't know sign language and began to panic. I had signed up for the workshop because some of the experienced storytellers at the North Shore Guild meeting highly recommended it. I hadn't stopped to consider my qualifications. The description on the Festival web page had sounded interesting:

> The objective of this workshop is to utilize the arts of storytelling and poetry in American Sign Language. The techniques used in the story or poem will be introduced. Participants will analyze the foundations of storytelling and poetry through theatrical games. There will be hands-on experiences such as

creating materials and combining them with ASL. Participants will be encouraged to explore their own style in their works.

The workshop was open and accessible to everyone.

The classroom was crowded when I opened the door but it was air-conditioned. (I wore a short-sleeved blouse over my tank top just in case it was cold.) The first thing that Peter did was to introduce himself in sign language but Donna Reiter Brandwein was there to interpret his sign into vocal language. I felt just a little bit better. When Donna was introduced, she explained her involvement with sign language this way. "I was just in love with words. The more I read, I realized that I was protecting myself from movement. Sign language gave me movement."

The participants in the workshop introduced themselves in both voice and sign. When it came to my turn, I admitted that I was ignorant when it came to sign language and how glad I was that Donna was there to interpret for us. I discovered that I wasn't the only one who didn't sign. Two other people were also without knowledge of sign language.

Peter told us that a knowledge of sign language wasn't necessary. His workshop would concentrate on expression, body language and gestures. I felt better.

Peter wrote the foundations of a story on the board: facial expression, body language, gesture and sign production. Without facial expression, a story is boring. And Peter told a story without expression.

(On Sunday morning, a local storyteller told a story during the Sacred Stories and Eulogies Hour. She lacked expression and movement in her telling. Although her story was interesting, the lack of expression and movement was similar to a piece of bread without the butter or jam.)

Peter explained that sign language is the deaf communities culture. That is what sets them apart.

We gathered in a circle and each participant was given a sign to express a word or emotion. I chose "confused." I had a hard time remembering the sign for the word. We spoke our sign many times, each taking a turn, going around the circle. We signed it HUGE, we signed it small, we signed it quickly, we signed it s.l.o.w.l.y. Each time we signed it with expression. The only part that I really got right was that I had to point to my head, the rest I'm still not sure of. I was blocked … my brain WAS NOT functioning. I blamed it on the heat.

Peter emphasized that facial expression is key. "Kids love to watch expression." He said it is important for children to see the full range of motion—the different possibilities to express one emotion: HAPPY—small smile ... large grin ... laughing ... dancing ... skipping ... jumping for joy....

Then we paired off and used our partner as a piece of clay, modeling an expression—Brave. The expression had to encompass the total being, arms, legs, shoulders, tilt of head as well as mouth and eyes. After we finished designing our creation, we toured the sculpture garden to view the sculptures of the other artists.

Most of the workshop was devoted to participation—volunteers expressing a story line. (I didn't volunteer ... my theatrical experience was limited to a small part in a first grade play. I think I was a duck.)

Everyone participated in the last production of the workshop. Peter divided us into groups—four in total. I was in group number four which was comprised of four people. Our assignment was to pick a hand character and use that character to tell a story. We chose the character "4" and decided to portray Peter's workshop. One of the girls said that every story needs a dog so she was the dog. It didn't matter that there wasn't a dog in our workshop. At first I thought that I would be the people coming to the workshop, it looked rather easy. The YOUNG girl who was directing our group soon made that part a bit more complex. I was soon LOST; I couldn't remember all the intricate hand movements that she was using. I think the members of my group gave up on me. I finally picked the part of the person who introduced Peter. The part was relatively easy, all I had to do was lecture, hand raised ... shaking up and down ... describe Peter's creativity ... draw a female form with my four fingers of each hand, and bring on Peter ... hand outstretched, palm up, moving from my body to the person next to me, who was very skilled in sign.

At 12:00, the Olio began with the featured tellers in the Family Tent. Jim May told the assembled group that because of the heat, ice cubes and sandwich bags to hold the ice would be available in ice chests at the back of all the tents during the afternoon.

Jim May announced that last year was the first year that signers were part of the National Storytelling Festival. They included two from the Illinois Storytelling Festival. With that he introduced Donna, who explained, "We are really interpreters rather than signers because we interpret for someone else." And the stories began.

This year I made it a point to talk to Shanta. I was tempted to last year but passed up the opportunity. I told her that she was the hook that pulled me into storytelling. When I mentioned that I was wearing a funny hat at the Art Institute, she remembered who I was. Shanta told me to keep my mouth moving, (to keep telling stories.)

As usual, I had trouble deciding who I wanted to listen to, so many stories, so many options, so little time. I started out in the adult tent listening to the Double Deckers.

Peter Cook was telling a story in the second half hour and I wanted to watch his story. Susan O'Halloran was the M.C.

I had just bought Susan's book on marriage fables and wanted to ask her permission to tell the stories.

I stayed in the adult tent to listen to Laura Simms, <u>The Gift Of Dreams</u>. Laura is a VERY, TALENTED teller. She has the ability to change the tone of her voice, becoming different characters. I knew that I would never be able to tell stories the way that she did and contented myself watching her style and enjoying her performance.

After Laura's performance, it was 3:45. I decided to attend 4:00 PM Mass at St. Peter's, even though it meant missing stories. As I walked down the path to church, two World War II planes flew overhead as a salute to the Tuskegee Airmen who were telling their stories in the Traditions tent. The Tuskegee Airmen where the first black fighter pilots in WWII. No one wanted to fly with them until the pilots discovered that they never lost a plane that they were escorting. Then everyone wanted to fly with them. Four or five men from the old squadron were at the festival in their dress uniforms. They stood tall, even though they were in their 80's.

I attended 4:00 PM Mass at St. Peter's. The reading from the gospel caught me by surprise. How often do we hear something that doesn't sink in, it flows through our mind without stopping? I had heard the story before. This time it stayed. I had learned that when problems surfaced that were too much for me to handle, I knew I couldn't walk on water but I could give the problem to the One who could. In the gospel Peter was walking on water. The thought that provided comfort was when Peter started to sink, he cried out "Lord save me! Immediately Jesus stretched out his hand and caught him and he said to him, 'O you of little faith, why did you doubt.'" Matthew 14: 27–32. Even though St. Peter surfaced regularly in my life: my parents were buried in St. Peter and Paul cemetery, I attended Mass at St. Peter's in Chicago's loop, I knew I COULD NOT walk on water, but I knew how to YELL "HELP!"

I was going to leave after Communion but the Communion song was <u>Come To The Water,</u> by John Foley. I returned to my pew for the third verse:

> And let all who toil, let them come to the water. And let all who are weary, let them come to the Lord. All who labor without rest, How can your soul find rest except for the Lord.

The song ended before all of the assembly had received Communion. The next song was <u>Let There Be Peace On </u>Earth, which was one of my father's favorites. I was glad that I had stayed for the full Mass.

I stopped at my car to get Susan O'Halloran's book. I found her right away at the selling tent. After she signed her book, I told her the story of Bear Butt, how as I finished each prayer, birds were present. She said we need these reminders when we are stuck for inspiration.

An olio finished the Saturday performance. Ghost stories would begin at 9:00 PM. It was only 6:00. I had time to find my motel, check in, wash up, get something to eat and come back for ghost stories.

I was given room 104, right next to the swimming pool. As I was getting my bags from the car, two cars pulled up and a group of women assembled. From their conversation I could tell that they were coming from the festival too. I spoke to them briefly before going to my room. I couldn't wait to get my clothes off and wash up. I was drenched from the heat of the day.

I was concerned that I would have trouble finding my way back to the festival in the dark. Night was descending quickly. I shouldn't have worried. I didn't have any trouble finding the turnoff even though there was no signal or stop sign to mark the intersection.

Jim May told the assembled crowd that despite the heat, 1000 people had attended that afternoon.

In 1998, the temperature in the evening had gotten quite cold. That didn't happen Saturday night. It cooled off but not enough for a sweater. I felt very tired. But the stories were very good and I didn't want to leave. Around 11:00 PM I decided to lie down on the grass and rest my eyes. I was amazed when I saw a band of circles in the sky. I hadn't noticed them in all the times I had looked at the stars. I was going to ask someone if they knew what the circles where, but I didn't want to interrupt the story being told. Which was just as well. After staring at the circles for a while, I realized that they were the lights from the park. I closed my eyes and listened to the story. I think I drifted off to sleep a few times. When the last teller started his story, I decided it was time for me to go. I was driving back by myself and tired, I didn't want to fall asleep at the wheel. I got a peach yogurt cone to wake me up. A man driving a cart offered me a ride to the parking lot. This time I accepted his offer. I was back at the hotel in ten minutes. And asleep soon afterwards.

Sunday morning, I opened the Gideon bible to Psalm 50, verse 4. "He shall call to the heavens from above, and to the earth, that he may judge his people."

I had time to exercise, eat, pack, read, and still arrive at the festival before the stories began at 10:00AM. I even stopped at the selling tent to buy a few CD's and tapes.

I saw the group of five women from the hotel. The earrings on one of the woman intrigued me. They were longer beaded loops than I had made. I asked Nan how she made them. Since Nan was from Minnesota, I think of them as Pipestone earrings. Ironically, after I found out how Nan made the earrings, I didn't see anyone from the group again.

The storytelling began; the session was devoted to Sacred Stories and Eulogies. A couple of comments from assorted storytellers during the session:

"Honoring the dead was a way of bringing God to the people."

"A person said that we created a small village during our festival."

"I think the privilege of telling stories and listening to stories opens up something in our hearts."

Connie Reagan-Blake told a story using a bouquet of flowers. Each different flower reminded her of a storyteller who has passed on and she described the person using the characteristics of the flower. After the session I asked her permission to use her idea of the flowers to tell a story. She said that our festival was the first time she told that story.

Connie said that she takes totems with her when she travels and when she does a recording. She needs a steamer trunk for all of her possessions. She likes to take no-face dolls, so children can add their own expressions.

"I always travel with flowers. I love my garden so much; I take part of it with me."

"I travel with rocks, my rock garden."

During Connie's last story of the session, she told how she was swapping stories with a friend at a school. While Connie sat on the end of the stage and listened to her friend tell a story, she felt the presence of her cat on her lap. She was very surprised, her cat was at home. She wondered if something had happened to her. She could feel the weight of the cat on her lap; she could feel her soft fur. She moved her attention back to her friend's story but every once and a while, she felt the presence of her cat on her lap. After the stories were finished, a teacher brought a boy to Connie's attention. She told Connie that the boy hadn't spoken a word for two weeks until during their stories, he turned to his teacher and said, "They're good aren't they?" The teacher went on to finish telling the boy's story. Two weeks before, the boy's house caught fire. The family got out but their cat didn't make it. Something in their stories opened or healed something in his heart. Connie doesn't know which cat's presence was in her lap, hers or the boys.

Shanta told a story of how the women in the village were given so much time to learn who they were and what they had to do. After they formed committees, talked the thing to death, got nowhere, they spent five days together not talking—joining their minds. And after a few days passed, they began to smile at one another, hug one another and after five days, they knew what their purpose was.

The Storyweavers lived on their twenty-eight acre farm on a mountain in Tennessee for twenty years before returning to Illinois. Their story had this theme. "Hide the truth—break it into tiny pieces and hide the pieces in each human heart. Then when the people find the truth in their own hearts, they will look for it in the hearts of others."

I went to the adult tent to listen to Shanta and Nyla Ching-Fuji. Nyla said that according to Hawaiian custom, every miscarriage is a fully developed child. Nyla told a story about a princess who had a miscarriage in the ocean; the baby became a shark and protected Pearl Harbor. The navy wanted to put a floating dry dock in the harbor, they tried three times. Each time when the last piece of concrete was poured, the dock collapsed. The navy finally consulted the Hawaiian elders and learned that they could build a floating dock, not one anchored by pilings.

In Hawaii, they feel that you need a village to raise a child. Every woman the same age as the child's mother is its mother; every grandmother is its grandmother. They call their grandmothers Tui Tui.

Nyla ended her set by saying, "Our history is our stories, it is not folk tales."

Then I went to listen to Bill Harley in the family tent. He had this advice for would be storytellers. "Baby stories are just like babies. You don't dare drop them, because if you do, you might never pick them up again."

Bill Harley introduced his part of the olio by saying, "This festival is a little jewel. You're insane to be here, you know it don't you but we're so glad that you're here."

"I travel all over the United States and there's nothing like this."

Bill finished his set with Pete Seeger's song If I had A Hammer. Most of the audience was up on their feet, swaying with the music, raising their hands, singing along.

Jim May remarked, "Did you see them over there, rippin up the sod, pounding the worms? You know the next storyteller can dance!"

Jim May told the story of his mother at the nursing home, the birthday card, the valentine card, her roommate. Neither of them remembered what they had for lunch. (Alzheimer's story.). His mother's birthday was Feb 8.

A cardinal sang as I pulled out of the parking lot. On the way home, I saw a hawk land on a telephone pole.

July 23, 1999 ... Friday evening as I prepared for bed, I read the following in the May-June issue of The Society of Children's Book Writers and Illustrators magazine.

If you dare to set out on a mountain,

And find you've somehow gone astray,

Though you miss your final destination,

Look at what you've learned along the way.

—Sandra Weber, verse from her song <u>The Love Of Ester Mountain.</u>

If our story was published when I first began looking for a publisher, I never would have discovered storytelling and look at all the fun I would have missed.

CUYLER, A SPECIAL FRIEND

Early in the afternoon I took Mabel, our daughter's seven-month Chocolate Labrador retriever for a walk. We were waiting to cross the street at a stoplight when Mabel saw a dog on the other side that she just knew was a new friend. Mabel couldn't wait to meet this dog and darted into the street, narrowly missing a turning car. Jerking her back, I proceeded to severely reprimand her. As the owner of the other dog passed us, she exclaimed, "Dogs don't understand English." I felt very sorry not only for the woman's dog but also for her two small children. And I thought of our friend Cuyler.

I considered writing his story for some time. I finally received the opportunity on March 18, 2000 at our camper. I find the timing to be very interesting. We were spending a week on vacation at the camper when Cuyler first joined our family fifteen years ago.

In the country, many towns have special weekends to honor events in their history. The weekend we adopted Cuyler, Amboy celebrated Depot Days, a remembrance of the time when the depot in their town was an important part of the Illinois Central Railroad, which ran between Freeport, IL and Clinton, Iowa. The festivities started Friday night with the opening of the carnival and a band. Saturday morning, the sidewalks were crowded with booths featuring craft items; a parade highlighted the afternoon followed by a pork chop supper and more entertainment at night. A pancake breakfast fed the crowd Sunday morning, giving them the energy to examine the hundreds of old cars that lined the streets for an old car show.

Sue, our youngest daughter, was 10, too young to stay in the city with her older brother and sisters who had summer jobs, so she came on vacation with us. She and I went to the craft show on Saturday. The local animal shelter had a booth showcasing animals that were up for adoption. A puppy in one of the cages caught Sue's eye. She asked if she could have it. A few weeks before, we had to have Rusty, our Irish Setter, put to sleep when arthritis caused him constant pain. Sue felt we had room for another dog. I reminded her that Shanae, a female Labrador—German Shepherd, and three cats were at home. Since we didn't lack for animal companions, I said no.

When we arrived back at the camper, Sue told her father about the puppy. She played on his sympathy and asked for a dog all her own. She told her father that although Shanae was supposed to belong to her oldest sister, Shanae had claimed Sue's brother as her person. Her father gave in. Sue and her dad went back to town to adopt the puppy. Two brothers waited in a cage. Although we were told that they were a mixture of Siberian husky and German shepherd, they didn't look alike. One looked like a bear, black, with long curly fur, very husky and energetic, his brother was smaller, a mixture of black and brown with a quieter disposition. Sue chose the quieter dog.

That night we chained the puppy up in the kitchen. He made so much noise crying, whining and barking that Dad told Sue to get her sleeping bag and sleep with her dog. Sue had a hard time naming him. He had very wobbly legs and fell over so often that Dad said she should name him Tequila. Sue ignored her father and chose the name Cuyler.

Cuyler was top dog for one week. Then he went home with us to meet the rest of the family. Shanae wasn't impressed with this small, yapping addition to the family. She had finally gained the status of top dog and didn't want to give it up. She body slammed him as she passed and knocked him into the post separating our double parlor. Cuyler didn't know what had hit him but Shanae clearly showed him who was boss. Cuyler followed her lead for 12 years.

He was very quiet when in the back yard by himself, but if Shanae was outside for back up, he was a very brave fellow. He never started to play with her, but was always willing to join in the fun. At first he loved to play tug of war but we didn't allow him to win very often so he lost interest. Although he would chase a ball his favorite toys where a squeaky green rubber frog and a rubber hamburger.

At first Cuyler loved to ride in the car. He was small enough to ride on the shelf by the back window. Then we took him to the vets to be dewormed, on the way home he threw up. Even though he grew too big to ride on the back shelf, he wasn't able to ride in the car without pills for motion sickness until he was in his teens.

One of Cuyler's favorite pastimes was eating. He was always willing to finish Shanae's food or the cats if he could reach it. He was willing to join anyone who was eating at any time, waiting patiently for his share. Most of the time he was very quiet, but he would become vocal if he felt left out.

My father, whom we called Pap, lived with us. Cuyler could always count on a hand out from him. He had all of us pegged. He knew that Dad and Sue's brother Bill were pushovers. He also knew that neither Sue nor I would give in to his sad gaze.

Both of the dogs were allowed on the furniture. Shanae shadowed Bill. When Bill was home, she was usually at his side unless something very interesting was happening. She spent her nights sleeping near his bed.

When we weren't home, Cuyler loved to sleep on our bed, pulling back the covers to expose the pillows on which he would lay his head. When the family was home, he had to be with everybody, unless he was tired. Often when the noise became too much for him, he would go into the shower in the first floor bathroom to sleep. At night, he took up a position near the second floor bathroom where he could monitor the comings and goings of his family. As he got older, he also preferred to lay behind Dad's chair, underneath the window, out of the way of the traffic. When the Christmas tree occupied that space, it was hard to figure out who felt the most displaced, Dad with the movement of his chair, or Cuyler. We had to be careful where we placed the presents because Cuyler was very determined to continue to occupy his space under the window.

After many years passed, Pap's memory began to decline as a result of Alzheimer's disease. Both dogs continued to join him for meals. As Pap's memory loss increased, he took more time to eat. Cuyler was able to join Dad, then visit Sue and I before finishing his meal with Pap. Pap always gave him something, even if it was only coffee. Cuyler didn't like coffee.

Since I had a full time job, Pap's freedom was curtailed when the disease progressed to the point where he had to spend his day at Day Care. He always petted both of the dogs before he left, telling them to guard the house.

One day, Pap didn't come home. He had fallen while at Day Care and was admitted into the hospital for observation. After four days, Pap lost his ability to walk and had to be admitted into a nursing home. That night when I came home, I found an unpleasant surprise on my side of the bed. Cuyler had left a big, smelly pile, expressing his displeasure at Pap's absence. Since Pap always left and returned with me, he knew who to blame.

Pap lingered less than a month in the nursing home. I wondered if Cuyler would give us more souvenirs when he passed over, but he had already expressed his feelings on the subject. The hymn <u>On Eagles Wings</u> permanently marked the day for our family. Soon after Pap's passing the stress of caring for my father and unpleasant working conditions dictated that I quit work.

Two years later, we noticed that Shanae was beginning to show her age. Always playful, she appeared to be losing her memory. To make matters worse, she seemed to have arthritis. Often she pestered Bill to go to bed. Bill climbed the stairs to his bedroom on the third floor and Shanae followed. Sometimes Bill would come back down, but Shanae wouldn't reappear until morning. She was tired; she was going to bed. When Bill brought his future wife home, Shanae didn't accept Michelle right away. She always managed to be in the middle, she pushed Michelle aside like she used to push Cuyler.

As time progressed, Shanae forgot to eat. Cuyler always ate her share, then ate more when I put more food down for her. In order to keep peace with the dogs, I always put down an extra smaller portion for Cuyler. Shanae lost weight that Cuyler put on, so much that he resembled a round sausage.

Walking up and down the stairs became a chore for her. Often we heard a thump, thump, thump that meant that Shanae was falling down the steps. For her safety, we put up a child's gate, restricting both dogs to the first floor.

Finally Shanae lost feeling and control in her back hips. In order to make sure that she did her business, I asked her permission to help her, then carried her down the back steps. That accomplished, I took both of the dogs for a walk. After again asking her permission to help her, I carried Shanae back up the stairs. I was concerned how we would manage once winter arrived. Even though she was now 16, we didn't want to put Shanae down while she still had a quality of life. I didn't need to worry.

The last week of October, Shanae became puppy-like, running and frisking through the house. She had energy when we went for a walk. She even did a head first somersault when an interesting smell attracted her attention.

Bill was always home on Sunday nights. This night was an exception. Bill drove Michelle home and it was so late he stayed over night at her house. Late in the evening on All Soul's day, November 2, Shanae had a stroke. She was in such howling pain that we took her to the emergency clinic and had her put down.

It was after 1:00 AM when we returned from the clinic. Even though the hour was late I was too upset to sleep. As I sat drinking a cup of warm milk, I received a great gift. I saw Shanae's spirit run through the house. I felt much better after that and was able to go to bed.

The next morning, I had to run an errand. Before leaving, I put away the child's gate; we didn't need it anymore. When I returned, Cuyler had expressed his displeasure at losing his companion. His extra weight didn't allow him to climb up onto the bed so he left his pile on the floor by my side of the bed.

We debated about getting another companion for Cuyler but decided against it. He was too reserved; we felt a new dog would take his spot as top dog. After everything that he had endured, we didn't want that to happen to him. We decreased his portion of food, trying to help him get his shape back. I continued to take him for walks until I noticed that arthritis was restricting his ability.

One winter day, the stairs had iced over during the night. I let Cuyler out and soon he was barking to come in. When I looked outside, I saw that he was down on the sidewalk instead of up at his normal spot by the back door. That was when I noticed the icy steps. Cuyler tried to climb the steps and fell back down. I walked to the front door to check those steps. They were icy too. A thick layer of snow prevented me from opening the cellar doors to the basement. I didn't know how I was going to get Cuyler into the house. When I returned to the back door, somehow Cuyler had made his way up onto the porch. Determination!

Through the years we had gradually lost most of our cats. Mickey was the last. She was very tiny, the size of a kitten and very timid and shy. She lived on the second floor of our house, only coming downstairs to eat. She had never been out of our house. She didn't realize that she was a cat and Cuyler was a dog. When she came into heat she threw herself all over him. Often putting her head in his mouth. Since the house had quieted down, Mickey began to spend more time on the first floor. One day I noticed a large growth on her stomach. Since she was such a timid cat, I decided to let nature take its course and kept her as comfortable as I could.

One February morning I found a smelly pile on the downstairs floor under the arch of our double parlor. I was puzzled, I didn't understand. Cuyler rarely went in the house. The next morning I understood. I found Mickey lying under the arch of our double parlor, headed for the kitchen to get something to eat. Cuyler expressed his feelings again, only this time, he knew before we did.

Cuyler's condition continued to deteriorate. Now he needed help getting up the stairs. He was really top dog. I arranged my schedule to accommodate his needs. We either made sure that someone was home for the weekend or took him to the camper with us.

We had an opportunity to go to South Dakota for a vacation. Bill, now married, offered to take Cuyler to his house. I told Bill that if Cuyler's condition worsened, he should put him down. When Sue and I arrived to pick up Cuyler, we couldn't find him at first. We didn't notice the note telling us that Houdini was in the garage. No matter how Bill tried to keep him in the kitchen, he always escaped. The garage was his last resort.

Our elm tree in the back yard survived the Dutch Elm disease, which killed all the elm trees in our neighborhood in the 60's. When we returned from South Dakota, a notice was on our door that the Asian Longhorn beetle had infested our elm. It was scheduled to be cut down in two days. Sue, Cuyler and I kept our tree company as it was cut down. The rings showed that it was 85 years old. It had the distinction of having the biggest base of any tree that they cut down in the city.

We knew that Cuyler's days were getting short. I had to help him down the stairs, and then I had to carry him back up. We had to block off the stairs so Cuyler couldn't go up to the second floor. Many times I had to get up in the middle of the night when his yelps for help woke me.

In the early morning hours of a Friday morning in September, Cuyler's yelps for help woke me. I went downstairs to help him up and waited for him to get settled again. He paced back and forth for over an hour. I finally helped him to lie down and went back to bed. That morning, after Cuyler had his morning walk and breakfast, I made sure he was comfortable before I left for church. On the way, I passed an old house that was being torn down. "It's about time," the neighbor said as she prepared to watch the destruction. Fr. Dennis chose <u>On Eagles Wings</u> to open the Mass. When I returned home, I helped Cuyler up. Then I took him outside. When we returned, Cuyler was once again pacing nervously. "Should I help you lay down?" I asked him. As I spoke those words I knew it was time to help him lay down for the last time. The time had come to allow him to join his friends on the other side.

Do dogs understand English? I think they understand more than we give them credit for.

One week later, our house was so quiet that neither my husband nor Sue could stand it. On Sunday, Sue brought Mabel home. From a house used to older dogs we now had an eleven-week toddler. Our house was no longer quiet.

TRAVELING LIGHT

Renaissance Court is an award winning senior center, which occupies a space in the old library building in downtown Chicago, now called the Cultural Center. It has a broad list of programs—classes are offered covering everything from dance and exercise, to drawing and painting, poetry, plays and writing. It was designed for Chicagoans 55 years of age and older and I was finally old enough to join.

When I attended a monthly meeting of the North Shore storytelling guild, I learned that a new program was beginning at Renaissance Court. They were putting together a list of entertainers to help people planning parties. Auditions were being held to secure a place on the list. A number of storytellers were invited to be on the list, some of the guild members were even on the judging panel. I asked if I should try out.

When my application was accepted, I learned that each act had ten minutes to show their talent. I planned my outfit and rehearsed my story. I decided to tell Pap and the Pancake Turner. By adding a few details, it timed out to ten minutes.

The day of the audition was a beautiful spring day, warm enough that I didn't need a coat. Normally when I tell stories I wear regular clothes but I decided to dress up for the occasion and wore a matching outfit: blouse, slacks and long overcoat in shades of blue. I felt very professional. My storytelling friends were not there; since they knew me, in fairness they removed themselves from judging.

I was amazed at the different costumes in the waiting room. I was glad I wasn't wearing normal clothes. Two or three groups were ahead of me—tap dancers, singers and musicians. I watched with interest as they carried their equipment into the room. I remembered the years when my husband was a square dance caller and we carried his equipment—turn table, speakers and records everywhere. I didn't miss toting equipment. A Girl Scout song suggested that you carry a smile in your pocket, ready to put it on at a moments notice. I imagined I carried my stories in my pocket, ready to be told when the occasion called for them. I introduced myself, and added, "I am a storyteller." I thought I told my story well and it was well received but it wasn't the type of story that people are used to hearing. It wasn't a folktale or a children's tale. In a couple of weeks I learned that I hadn't made the entertainment list.

In the summer Tom and I went to Hawaii. We spent a couple of days in Oahu, then flew to Kauai, the garden island. Kauai is a very small island. Mountains are in the center, the roads are close to the ocean but they only go three quarters around the island. Each day we listened to the weather, then decided if we were going to visit the north or the south side of the island. We put more than 240 miles on our car.

Many of my friends knew that I collected rocks on my travels. They warned me not to take rocks home from Hawaii. It was bad luck.

Each morning, the rooster's crow woke me in time to greet the rising sun on the beach. In the course of the ten days we remained on the island, I told the story of Pap and The Pancake Turner three times. The first morning I found a rock that resembled a turtle. I looked around for someone who could tell me if it was a rock or coral. I was very happy when Sue, a first grade teacher from Oregon, told me that it was a piece of coral, shaped by the sand, rocks and water. I could take it home. As we talked, she mentioned that she had just lost her sister. I told her the story of Pap and The Pancake Turner.

That was the beginning of my coral collection. Each morning as I watched the rising sun, I looked for coral. I found one that reminded me of a poodle or a butterfly depending on how you held it. The last day on the island, a coral with raised arms washed in on the waves.

There is a custom in Hawaii to honor the place a person dies; the area is marked by crosses and flowers. One day we drove down a sugar cane road, looking for a waterfall. As we turned onto the road, I noticed a cemetery at the base of a hill. Stones outlined the graves and I was intrigued: I told my husband I wanted to stop to take a picture on our return. As we drove down the clay road I was very surprised when in the middle of the sugarcanes, we came across a place were a child died. Balloons, toys and flowers decorated the area.

Returning from the waterfall we stopped at the small Immaculate Conception cemetery. There was a distinct difference in the graves, half were outlined in stones, the rest only had a grave marker. I saw an older man tending a raised stone grave and wandered over to ask a few questions. I learned the cemetery was separated into two sections. In the older section, the grave could be outlined with stones, while in the newer section, only a grave marker was permitted. James said his wife had passed away the previous year and he came every day to tend her grave. I shared <u>Pap and The Pancake Turner</u> with him.

A grave caught my attention in a corner of the cemetery. It looked like it belonged to a child. Toys and balloons and flowers and pinwheels and children's chairs and tables were everywhere. The older man told me the story of the occupant of the grave. It belonged to a three-year-old boy who was killed during a race on the cane road up above. The car flipped over and the child went through the windshield. I asked him to share the story with the grieving family. Before we left the cemetery, I took a few pictures of the child's grave.

A few days later, I was concerned about the pictures I had taken at the cemetery. I asked my husband if we could visit again. This time the grandmother of the child was at the cemetery. They had celebrated the child's birthday, complete with balloons, ice cream and cake the week before. Once again, I shared <u>Pap and The Pancake Turner.</u>

PROJECT ACTIVE

(Project Active was a program run by a health organization designed to help people become more active. Our church announced a session was starting in September before school in the morning. Since I was an early riser and needed to lose weight, I decided to attend. Each week, we had homework. We received a handout to read about the topic covered in class with questions to answer. I wrote this essay as an answer. It surfaced while I was putting together the stories for this book.)

The homework for week 7 was titled Recruiting My Support Troops. Although we didn't have to fill out all the blanks, we were instructed to think through the questions.

1. What do I need help with?

2. Who could help me?

3. How could they help?

4. How would I ask for their help?

5. How could I reward them for helping me?

I knew I would have trouble with the assignment. I have trouble asking for help unless I'm either swamped with work or don't have the skill needed for the task. I think that my independent nature is one of the things responsible for the ongoing "help" that I receive. The events of Thursday are a perfect example of this "help."

Following the Project Active meeting, I attended 8:30 AM Mass. During the homily, Fr. Jason asked the seventh and eighth graders how their parents showed that they loved them. He also asked if we experience Jesus' love in our lives. He ended his homily by asking if we do things because it is the right thing to do or are our actions done for the benefit we will receive.

I was going to the Field Museum to view the Kremlin Gold exhibit. Members had a chance to preview the exhibit before it opened to the public. I had requested tickets for 10:30, 11:00 or 1:00. Because of vacation, I sent the request in late and didn't receive my tickets by mail. I didn't know which time I had been given.

Before catching the train, I stopped at the auto repair garage to talk to the mechanic about the newest problem I had noticed with my car. It was hesitating before accelerating. I was worried that I might be having trouble with the drive train or the transmission. I planned to make a hundred mile drive and was apprehensive. The mechanic told me that he would take the car for a test drive. I arranged to bring it by on Friday morning.

As I approached the "L" station, I watched the train pull out. I wasn't pleased. I was concerned that I wouldn't get to the museum by 10:30. It was already 9:30.

When I reached the top of the stairs I was surprised to see one of my neighbors. I was glad to see her, I had thought of her that morning. I knew she would know how J.B. was. He was an elderly dog who was having trouble walking. I knew he was living on borrowed time. My suspicions were confirmed when I learned that on top of his other problems J.B. had cancer on his nose that was interfering with his breathing. His owner had him put to sleep.

I enjoyed riding with my neighbor to Belmont where we both got off to transfer to the subway. I was going downtown; she was going to visit a friend in a nursing home in Des Plaines. When I commented on the length of her journey, she replied that she had missed the bus which would have taken her to the train and needed to take a longer route.

The red line train was packed. An elderly man offered me his seat. I felt bad taking it but he insisted.

I arrived at Roosevelt road a little bit after 10:00. As I waited to cross the street, a girl asked the time. It was 10:07. I figured I could easily walk to the museum before 10:30.

When I reached the membership desk, I learned that I had been given a ticket for 1:00. The attendant asked if I had seen Endurance, the story of an explorer's trek across the South Pole. I asked if they had tickets to Star Wars. I had missed the preview when the exhibit opened. She had a ticket for 9:00. I was told that it was still good.

I went downstairs and was surprised to find myself at the exhibit entry. Star Wars—The Magic Myth—based on an ancient form of mythology—the "hero's journey." As I read the placards comparing the myth to Star Wars, I was surprised at the parallels to my life.

The Wise And Helpful Guide. "Often the inexperienced hero finds he cannot proceed without supernatural aid, in the form of a 'wise and helpful guide.'" I thought of the help I receive from my father since he has passed over.

The Threshold, "The hero must leave his familiar life behind to begin a journey ... from childhood to adulthood and to a life transformation." My life has certainly changed since I quit work after my father's passing. I have experienced changes that I would never have dreamt possible, the most notable being that I'm no longer make mountains out of molehills in the space of a second.

Into the Labyrinth, "a labyrinth has always symbolized a difficult journey into the unknown."

The Dark Road Of Trials, "Midway through the hero's journey comes a long and perilous path of trails, tests and ordeals that bring important moments of illumination and understanding. Again and again along the way, monsters must be slain and barriers must be passed." Another passage that I could relate to, very well.

The Sacred Grove, "The 'sacred grove' is another mythic motif; it represents an enclosure where the hero is changed. Ancient peoples widely believed the tree to be infused with creative energy. Forests came to symbolize mystery and transformation, and they were home to sorcerers and enchanters. Forests can also symbolize the unconscious mind, where there are secrets to be discovered and perhaps dark emotions or memories to be faced."

I hadn't realized that I was in a forest or that I had left until I attended an author's presentation. A young girl remarked that you don't know how far into the forest you have gone until you try to get out. I didn't realize how far out of the forest I had come until I heard questions asked by people that I myself would have asked a short time before. I realized that I had "left the forest."

The Path To Atonement, "The hero's journey sometimes includes a 'father's quest.' After many trials and ordeals, the hero finds his father and becomes 'at-one' with him. The process is called atonement.'" My mother died when I was four. I recently realized that she continued to be involved in my life after she passed over. She was just more skilled in hiding her "help" than my father was.

She allowed me to believe that I was doing things myself. My father was just so happy to regain the use of his faculties; he wanted to share the good news with me.

Sacrifices, "The opening of the mind and heart to spiritual knowledge requires a sacrifice from the hero."

The Hero's Return, "The 'hero's return' marks the end of the 'road of trials.' The hero must return from his adventure with the means to benefit his society."

Masks, "Are often part of the mythical ritual. They strike fear into the hearts of enemies, summon ancestors, or invoke supernatural beings."

I left the exhibit at 11:55. Enough time to grab lunch. After looking at the offerings at the Corner Bakery, I decided to eat at McDonald's. Once again I took the right staircase. This time arriving at the bottom in time to help a confused elderly man find McDonald's.

I had a half-hour before my ticket to Kremlin Gold. I chanced upon an exhibit of Kachina Dolls. I was familiar with the term. I knew that the Hopi Indians often wore masks representing a Katsina during their ceremonies. "A Katsina is the spirit of a living thing or the spirit of an ancestor who has died and become a part of nature. A Katsina is a spirit messenger, helper and friend who moves between the Hopi world and the supernatural world…. But a new Katsina may appear at any time. The four cradle dolls in the case may represent new Katsinam. They combine the faces of Teenager Mutant Ninja Turtles with the traditional bodies, thereby integrating the outside world into the Hopi world.'"

While I looked at the exhibit, I noticed many security guards speeding down the aisle. I was curious. I didn't have long to wait. I overheard a remark from one as he passed. Evidently they had found a child crying, he had gotten lost in the museum.

1:00—my trip to Russia began. Many religious goblets, Icons and crosses where included in the display as well as a portrait of Christ said to have miraculously appeared on linen cloth. Mary, Mother of Jesus played an important part in the Russian religion. Her image adorned not only Icons but was reflected in jewelry.

As I wandered through the exhibit, I overheard a husband asking his wife if she was dawdling again. I laughed, although my husband wouldn't have used that term, it was a comment that he would have made. I took the opportunity to exchange a few words with the woman. I remarked that my husband wouldn't have the patience for my poking, which is why I came alone. I overheard them arrange to meet near Sue, the new dinosaur, at a specific time.

I left the exhibit at 2:55. I poked quite a bit.

I stopped at the museum store. I treated myself to a lemon bar at the Corner Bakery, managing to get my hands sticky. Not wanting to have sticky hands all the way home I stopped in the bathroom. I was chiding myself for not writing down the expression the husband had used when the woman came into the bathroom. This time I wrote the expression down. We exchanged a few more comments. Specifically about viewing the exhibits with our husbands. "I don't let him cramp me," she said. "I always take my time."

As I walked back to the subway, I was at the right place, at the right time to direct a couple to the aquarium.

I felt bad that I had left our dog alone all day. The subway train must have been late. We sped through the underground, arriving at Belmont station in 10 minutes. The brown line train was waiting.

On the way home, I met another neighbor whose dog was afflicted with arthritis.

The answers to the questions.

1. What do I need help with? Everything!

2. Who could help me? Although I appreciate the help I receive from other human beings. I am constantly "helped" by my friends in high places. I overheard a woman remark after church one Sunday, "I have learned that I'm always where God wants me to be." I have shared some of the same learning. The lessons are repeated until I learn the lesson.

3. How could they help me? I don't understand how it works, but I have learned to walk with awareness.

4. How would I ask for their help? I just ask. When I first started to receive "help", I resisted. I waged quite a battle, with the word surrender popping up regularly in my life. I have since learned that resisting is not in my best interest. I trust that God or Mary is giving the directions.

5. How could I reward them for helping me? I remember to say, "thank you". I try to be aware of what is going on around me. I try to do the best I can with each day. Many times I'm in a place to tell a story to someone or help in some other way. I have come to realize that I have gone on a journey without leaving home. I don't know the purpose of this journey but I like this quote

by Dr. Rachel Naomi Remen, "An unanswered question is a good traveling companion, it keeps your eyes on the road."

6.   How does Jesus show He loves me? Although my waters do get very stormy at times, I'm amazed by the timing of an ordinary day, how much information I'm given if I'm open to accept it, how often I'm in the right spot to help someone if I'm walking with awareness.

Postscript added at 8:30 AM Sunday morning 10/22, after 7:30 Mass at Our Lady Of Perpetual Help

During Mass a teenage girl fainted, falling out of the pew onto the floor. The mother instantly rushed to Katie's aid, as did three other parishioners. Katie quickly returned to consciousness and was helped outside by her mother.

This episode reminded me that not only had I not documented the help that I received on October 10th when my car broke down but I neglected to call attention to the help the lost child received in the museum from more than four security guards. I'm not the only person who is watched over by our heavenly Father. We all are, we just need to ask for His help.

Monday morning, October 9th, Yom Kipper, the Jewish Day of Atonement, my husband returned to work after a two-week vacation to learn the company he worked for had been sold. Rumors spread through the company like wild fire—plant closings, early retirement, etc. My car had sat idle while we were gone. I had many errands to run and was very surprised when my car didn't start—the battery appeared to be dead. I contacted the garage to pick up my car. I knew my husband would be very tired after just returning to work and wouldn't want to deal with my car's dead battery.

That night both my husband and I had nightmares. Mine were many; his was easier to relate. He was driving a tractor-trailer truck down the road when many rocks blocked his passage; he had to swerve into the opposite lane to continue his journey.

Tuesday I picked up my car from the garage. They had replaced the battery, changed the oil, noticed that I had a cracked window washer reservoir and had a valve cover that was leaking oil.

Since none of the things that they discovered required immediate fixing, I started my car and headed off to do my errands. I traveled south where I ran into road construction. It took five light changes to travel one block, all the time the idling of my car was very rough. I didn't remember it being in that state the last time I drove it. I should have returned to the garage but hindsight is twenty-twenty. I turned right on Addison, heading for the expressway. I wanted to go to a store that was ten miles away. I continued to hit every red light, five in all. The idling on my car never smoothed out, it remained very rough until at the stop light at Sacramento and Addison my car shut off. I couldn't get it started again. Although it wasn't rush hour, traffic was already heavy. Horns were blowing impatiently at the delay. I decided to push my car to the side, in the bus stop.

A green car passed on my right side. Instead of going around, I watched in amazement as the driver went up on the grass next to the sidewalk. She got out, cell phone in hand. I thanked her for the use of her phone but said I wanted to get my car out of traffic first. She opened the passenger door to help push. A red sports car came to a quick stop behind me. A young man got out, walked to the rear of my car to push. They suggested I get in and steer, saving my weak wrists from further damage. A van stopped diagonally in the right hand lane, blocking traffic and allowing us safe passage. As quickly as they arrived, they were gone. As I stood on the side, a green van stopped to help. The driver said that she had seen me when she was traveling on the opposite side of the street, by the time she turned around I had already received assistance. She offered further help. Did I want to use her cell phone? Could she give me a ride? I thanked her for offer preferring to stay with my car.

My experience was a gentle reminder that I'm always watched over. I shouldn't spend my time worrying about things over which I have no control.

The garage had neglected to reset the computer on my car. The next day, I still had more car trouble but I was more aware. This time it was a loose fan belt and the fuel regulator need to be replace. As I prepared to go to the country for the weekend, my car needed the oxygen regulator replaced and the linkage for the shifting of the transmission had become disconnected.

Just as I have to be aware of the needs of my car for fuel and air, I need to be aware of the same need for my body. I have to remember to drink 64 ounces of water daily, eat good food and provide plenty of oxygen by doing deep breathing regularly. I need to remember this quote from *Queen Of Angels*. "Today when anxiety assaults me, I will stop, breathe in God's love, slowly exhale my gratitude and remember I am not in control, God is and I trust Him completely."

The week that I was having so much car trouble, my oldest daughter commented, "It doesn't look like you are supposed to go anywhere." It sure appeared that way but I must admit that I didn't stay home. I took my youngest daughter's dog, Mabel, for a long walk. I borrowed my husband's car to do the errands. I accepted an offer from a friend to car pool to a storytelling Guild meeting that was held in a northern suburb. I would not have found the house by myself in the dark.

It is my habit to begin the day opening the bible at random to pick my word for the day. This morning I opened to 2 Timothy 1:3. "I thank God, whom I serve, as my forefathers did, with a clear conscience, as night and day I constantly remember you in my prayers." I am in the habit of praying for everyone in the morning. At night I say thank you for the many blessings and "help" that I received during the day.

I have gotten into the habit of reading the whole chapter that my word comes from. Further in the chapter I read, "God has called us to a holy life.... not because of any thing we have done but because of his own purpose and grace.

I also read *Queen Of* Angels each day in the same manner. This morning: "Those who know God realize the folly of man's decisions without the light of divine grace."

Father's homily at Mass this morning reflected on the difference between God's will and man's ways. He told a story of an auto repair shop that was successful because the owner spent hours and hours under the cars of other people, giving service. Father suggested that God is asking us to live our lives as any successful business is run—giving service to others.

The events of the preceding days and the messages that pop up in my life on a regular basis lately would have sent me into a panic in days of old. But I have learned to trust God's plan for me, and leave the planning in his hands. Old habits die-hard though, I still try to drive the car on occasion.

PROJECT ACTIVE—EPILOGUE

Monday, October 23, 2000 8:30 AM

The weather this weekend was very nice—blue skies, sunshine, temperatures in the 70's. I was away from home, in the country. Today, I'm in the city, the sky is grey, the temperature is in the 60's, the forecast is for rain. It is easy to be depressed on a day like today.

I know that changes are in the wind. My youngest daughter is getting married; she will move out and take her dog with her. My husband's company has been bought. What changes to our life will that bring? Will he be offered an early retirement? Will they provide a pension plan? Even if he continues to work until he is 65, retirement is looming on the horizon.

Will our house be too big or too expensive for us to maintain? Should we sell our house? Should we purchase something else in the Chicagoland area? The questions continue.

It is easy to recognize that I am receiving help from above when three people stop to help when my car has broken down, and when a fourth person appears after the other three have gone. It is harder to recognize the help that I receive on an ordinary day.

ICE STORM

Our son, Bill, really likes ham sandwiches. Boiled ham was on sale on Thursday in January when I went grocery shopping; I bought a pound. By Saturday, most of the ham was gone. I decided to go to the store to buy more. I was afraid that if I waited it would be sold out.

Once outside, I began to regret my decision. Rain had turned to ice, covering the sidewalks, and my car. I debated—go to the store or go inside. I was able to open the car door, then the thin layer of ice came off the windows. The streets were salted and the store was close to home, on a main street. I was already outside. I decided to go to the store.

A bus pulled away from a bus stop as I approached the store. I watched in amazement as a tiny older man, walking with two canes, held up by a younger woman, crossed the street, and headed for the store. I watched in disbelief as the odd couple slipped and slide across the store parking lot. I parked my car; shoe skated across the icy pavement and entered the store myself.

The store wasn't busy. The weather had kept most people home. I was in luck. A large chunk of ham was in the delicatessen case, so I bought two more pounds. Next I met a neighbor and spent a few minutes in conversation. Before heading for the checkout line, I looked over the fresh vegetables. As I reached for an apple, the whole display avalanched onto the floor. Picking up the apples, I decided to leave the store before something else happened.

The checkout line wasn't long, only one person ahead of me. I was surprised when the elderly man I saw crossing the street got in line behind me. I thought of the ice, the fun I had crossing the parking lot on two good legs and asked him if he wanted a ride home. When he accepted, I asked where his companion was. I was surprised when he said he didn't have one.

The woman was a stranger, already on the corner when he got off the bus, she offered a helping arm and he gladly accepted.

I drove my car up to the door of the supermarket and watched as the man entered, almost reclining on the seat. In a thick Irish brogue, he explained that he just had both hips replaced. He didn't know why he decided to go to the store and navigate the icy sidewalks. He only needed a couple of things.

When I drove him home, I learned that he took two buses to get to the store. As I deposited him at his doorstep, he told me that angels were watching over him. I believed it!

Sometimes at church, the homilies fit my life. Because they don't stay in my memory, I take notes. Sunday was no exception. Our pastor told us, "Jesus had a vision of life. He saw God as a very compassionate person. I don't think Jesus even realized he was taking risks. I think he was driven by the love of people to reach out. We should ask ourselves, what are the risks in our lives that Jesus would want us to take?"

Thinking about my trip to the store on Saturday, the first time I offered a complete stranger a ride home, I had to laugh.

AN INTERRESTING MEETING

There is something about a warm sunny spring day after a long, grey winter that makes a person need to be outside. It was just such a day when I met Leah. I had a lot of work to do inside the house but the sunshine beckoned. It was too early to plant flowers. I didn't have grass seed. It wasn't warm enough to sit and drink a cup of coffee but I was determined to be outside. I decided to rake up the winter debris from the front yard. It seemed our house was the gathering spot for all the leaves and paper in the neighborhood.

As I worked I noticed a tall, thin, elderly African American woman walking down the street. She was strangely dressed. Her hat was pulled down over her ears, hiding part of her face as well as her hair. A black leather trench coat hung down to the sidewalk, held together by a scarf for a belt. I couldn't help but watch her progress. I wondered if she was homeless. As she passed me, she stopped to talk and rest.

I learned she lived about five miles from our house in an apartment complex. She liked to walk and went for a long walk every day. I offered her something to drink, a cup of coffee or water. Both of which she refused.

Her name was Leah. She was 82 years young. I couldn't help notice her teeth; they were ground down to nubs. I found her fascinating. She said our yard always looked so neat and that I must be caught up on all my housework. I had to laugh. I admitted that housework had never been a love of mine. Our house was comfortably cluttered, reasonably clean.

I learned she was the oldest of 18 children who never married or had children of her own. She was "raised up in Louisiana." Her mother was always calling her to clean the house or wash the clothes. She never learned how to cook. She didn't want children or a man running her. I told her that since she was the eldest, she probably had to look after all of her younger brothers and sisters. I understood why she wouldn't want to have children of her own. She had already raised enough.

We talked awhile longer then she went on her way. I offered to give her a ride home but she refused and I watched her walk away.

I thought—what a remarkable woman. As I watched her, I thought of my own mother. I didn't know very much about her. It hurt my father too much to talk about her. Every once in a while one of my aunts commented that I was like my mother, but they never went into details. I didn't know any of her stories. After my mother's passing, I was never able to get really close to another woman. Thinking of her, I realized how much my mother had given me. She hadn't abandoned me but saved my life. A line from scripture that I had heard many times before finally made sense, something about giving your life for a friend. I'd never really thought about it that way. I don't remember feeling guilty that I caused her death or that I was alive, but I missed having a mother. I thought of all the people whose mothers were living. I'm sure many were really great but there were the others, like Leah's, who had given birth to their children but never mothered them. I wondered how many people were carrying loads of guilt because of their relationship with their mother. Mother's Day has always been sad for me. That changed after I met Leah.

HAND OF GOD

It started innocently enough, with a phone call, from my daughter-in-law. The day after Christmas I asked her if she had gone shopping and what bargains she found. She shared her discovery; Joann Fabric's had marked their Christmas village houses down 75%.

When I was young, my aunt had a Christmas village of a few houses, children skating on a pond and others building a snowman on her dining room buffet. I always wanted a village of my own but the houses where expensive and other things were more pressing.

But 75% off? I had to investigate. I was surprised that the original price on the houses was much less than I had expected. The highest cost was $30. 75% off made them fit into my budget. I came home with 10 houses and a church, which I set up under our now empty Christmas tree. The houses looked great, books under the snow elevated them to a mountain village rather than a flat plain. But something was missing. The streets were too quiet, they were deserted, there were no people.

Numerous trips back and forth brought trees to the village and people walked the streets. My husband watched my creation grow with interest and laughter. He joined me on one of my trips to see what was available. That is when my project turned into a shared venture. We left the shop with 15 more houses. The possibility of staying under the Christmas tree had ended. The new village sprung up on the dining room table. Numerous trips to distant Joann Fabric stores added to the village. We knew that the following year, a new design and space had to be used.

We wound up with two villages: a Victorian village springs to life on our dining room buffet. Horse drawn carriages travel the streets, modern conveniences are missing. In the next room, the mountain village spreads out.

With the help of shelves, books and boxes, the stores and houses scale the mountain. There is never enough room for all of the buildings.

I should have known something was going to happen. I had received a hint, but I hadn't understood. On New Year's Eve in 2005, at 4:30 in the morning a crash woke me, followed by glass tinkling. My husband and I searched the house from top to bottom looking for the cause. I thought I found the source of the noise in the attic when I saw two cabinet doors lying on the floor. But that wouldn't account for the glass tinkling. No windows were broken. Everything was fine in the basement. In the pantry, everything was as it should be. Finally the cause of the noise became apparent, the top two sections of my Christmas village were gone—6 buildings, trees and people where no longer on the top of the mountain.

A few days later, I drove my car to the Salvation Army to drop off clothes. During the drive, I noticed the temperature gauge moving to high and staying there. Recently the thermostat had been replaced; I wondered what could be causing the high temperature? Parking the car, I noticed a puddle of green tinged water under the car's engine. After dropping off the clothes, I abandoned the rest of my errands and drove to our mechanic's garage where I put my old car in their hands. I was hoping for a broken hose, but things were a bit more serious. Inspection revealed that my car needed a new head gasket, a repair that would cost several hundred dollars. Although my car was more than 10 years old, replacing it was not an option, neither was giving it up. We weren't ready to be a one-car family.

I thought the village avalanche was hinting at the problems with my car. I should have realized we weren't done, after all two shelves fell.

One morning in the middle of January, we woke to a world of white. More than 6 inches of snow had fallen during the night and more was on its way down. I promised my husband that I would only sweep the steps and leave the sidewalks for him. I knew our snow blower would make the task easier. It would save his back and my wrists. And it did. My husband not only plowed the sidewalk in the back yard, he included our whole alley and the entire front sidewalk on our side of the block. When the snow finally stopped, he repeated the process. Using the snow blower caused no damage to our bodies, or so I thought, until my husband used the bathroom and was surprised by a commode full of blood. I wasn't very worried. Especially when the bleeding didn't reoccur. I thought he strained something.

A couple of days later, we stopped at our favorite restaurant for breakfast after church. A friend had just returned from a trip to Minnesota with her eighty year old mother. The trip didn't turn out as the daughter had hoped. I listened as she described how her mother had become sick on the train, and was too ill to walk. She detailed the help she received getting her mother off the train and to the hospital. Her mother had pneumonia and lost the ability to walk during the hospital stay. Her mother had been living in a senior apartment but because of her illness and inability to walk, had to move to assisted living. The custodian for the senior building mentioned that her mother had become more forgetful before the trip and required more of his help on a daily basis. Her mother was very angry with her, as if her illness was her daughter's fault. As we talked, I mentioned that she shouldn't feel guilty; she had just seen the hand of God.

It was as if I was hit on the head. I realized we had seen the hand of God in the blood in the commode. The next day I made an appointment with our doctor. He didn't waste time, but made an appointment for my husband to have a colonoscopy at the hospital the following week.

The day before the test was not an easy one for my husband. Not only could he not have anything to eat, but he had to drink a lot of clear fluid and drink a mixture from the drugstore at prescribed intervals. The following morning, he was hungry. We decided that after his test we would go out for breakfast.

That breakfast didn't happen. He had only been gone for a short time when a doctor came into the waiting room and called my name. He headed for an office and I followed. "This is never easy," he said as he sat down, and I knew we were in trouble. I was right. My husband had a 90% blockage of his colon. Because of the mass, the doctor wasn't able to get his scope past it. Since my husband was already cleaned out, the doctor suggested he stay in the hospital and have the obstruction removed and I agreed.

I hoped the doctor would explain the problem to my husband. I was wrong. The nurse told me that my husband was awake, hungry and ready to leave. It was left up to me to break the news. And a long day became longer.

THE GREAT DEBATE

Normally an argument or a debate will involve two or more people. This debate is different. I am involved in a debate with the Director of my life. It is not the first time that I have been in this position and probably not the last. I have learned that it is easier to go or do as I'm directed, so I don't usually protest. But there are times when my stubbornness rises and I dig in my heels, refusing to move.

It would be easier if I received clear directions—written or spoken. I do, but they don't come clearly like I'm talking to you. They come through family, friends, the radio, newspapers, books, homilies at church, chance meetings with strangers, dogs or birds, sometimes even my own mouth. I'm left to interpret their meaning.

The current debate revolves around the writing of another book. Every time the idea surfaces, I find a reason why it isn't time to start. Or I ask a question concerning the project. My favorite is, "Why should I write another book?" Asked silently or loudly for the world to hear.

The answer or reply comes either that day or the next. A friend told me how much she enjoyed reading our story. She liked the way it is a family affair. She has passed it on to others who are dealing with Alzheimer's. She said it might help them. Kathy's mother-in-law picked up the book, hoping it would put her to sleep. It didn't. Terri, my middle daughter, finally read the book, ten years after her grandfather died. She laughed, she cried, she enjoyed the reading.

Another of my objections is the cost of self-publishing. I remind the powers that be that I quit my paying job in 1995, my husband is retired and costs of self-publishing have risen. The next morning I open to a passage in the bible that refers to the worth of a sparrow or the elegance of the flowers in the field. I'm reminded that I'm always taken care of.

I counter with the limited number of copies of *To Pap, With* Love that have been sold. Then I learn how people who have my book have passed it to friend after friend after friend.

Sometimes the answer comes from a bird or the radio. In 2003 my husband and I toured the National Parks in the West in our motor home. We were at Bryce canyon the first time I turned on the radio. I heard, "From a distance, God is watching you." We were at the tallest spot in Bryce where Golden eagles play in the wind current. We turned off the radio and got out of our motor home to enjoy the view. When we returned to the motor home, I turned on the radio again. I heard, "He will call my name."

After visiting Mesa Verde National Park, we stopped for evening Mass in Durango, Co. The music was simple, a couple sang accompanied by a guitarist. One of the songs caught my attention. After Mass I complimented the group on the music and learned the title of the song was The Wings that Fly Us Home. Our trip was over, we were heading to New Mexico to visit relatives, before going home.

I won't bore you with all the details. Lets just say that the homilies at the various churches we attended and the music played, reminded me of the task at hand. Be Not Afraid or On Eagles Wings, both favorite songs of mine accompanied us on our trip.

Driving back from New Mexico, a hawk flew across our windshield, so low I thought we were going to hit it. I turned on the radio and heard the words of a song, "You have just seen the hand of God."

In 2005, on the feast of the Epiphany, a friend told me at church that she dreamt I was writing a new book, spiritual in nature, which would help others. I was already involved in the battle about the new book so her dream didn't surprise me until she said that my words would go around the world. I have to admit that took my breath away. That day I received an e-mail from a distant cousin who just learned of my existence and book from another. I gave him several options to obtain the book. When he received the book, I was surprised to learn he lived in Sweden. His next e-mail mentioned that he liked my stories, because they concerned important aspects of life.

After many of these prompts, I sat down at the computer and wrote the first story of the new book. I was disappointed with the results. Whatever ability I had to write was gone. The words were stiff, stilted.

I read an article by an author in which he said that he liked to reread the writing of some authors whose style he admired. One author mentioned was Rex Stout who brought Nero Wolfe to life. He liked his style. I had to agree. I liked Nero Wolfe too, had more than 30 of his books and often reread them. After I read the article, I picked one of Rex Stout's books from my library. Without looking at the copy-write on the book, I could tell that it was an early story. The writing was good but the characters and the descriptions were not as polished as the later stories. Soon after a friend told me she was rereading my book for the third time.

I began 2005 with more directions. Our priest's New Year's Day homily ended with the question: "What gift do you have that will reveal God to others? You have a unique place in God's plan. If you choose not to do it, it's not going to get done." At breakfast at our favorite restaurant, another priest who was no longer at our parish asked if I was still writing.

To add a bit of frosting to the day, our dog brought a stuffed animal downstairs while we were at church. It is a white lynx with brown spots, which was up on a dresser. A beanie baby born close to my birthday, its name is Tracks, a name I've thought of using for a title.

In March I read that a class on memoir writing was starting at the Renaissance Center: Me, Myself and I directed by Beth Finke. I thought it might help my writing and decided to attend.

At the first session I learned that Beth had received an award for an essay that she wrote about a Sox game. Blind, she brought a different vision to the game.

And out of my own mouth came the reason why I should write our stories. I look at a situation with different eyes and help people to realize that they are not alone. The song Be Not Afraid keeps surfacing. When will I begin? Good-question.

BETH'S PARTY

The forecast was the same: high near ninety, with a chance of thunderstorms. A weatherman commented, "This is the hottest it has been in two years and summer hasn't started yet". What a great forecast for the Printers Row bookfair and the Blues Festival at Grant Park.

Beth Finke was hosting a panel on memoir writing at noon on Saturday at Printers Row, with a party afterwards. I planned to attend. I spent the winter with her in a memoir writing class that she mentored at Renaissance Court.

God is the Boss of my life and my plans often make the Boss laugh. I planned to leave the house at 11:00, allowing enough time to arrive before the presentation began. My Floridian daughter phoned at 10:45. Three weeks ago, a woman stepped on her gas pedal instead of the brakes hitting Terri's 2005 red mustang convertible from behind when Terri stopped for a stalled car on the expressway. The resulting collision left Terri with a severe whiplash, back pain and knee problems. By the time I listened to her newest round of doctors and therapy, it was later than I planned to leave. Trains came quickly, they moved rapidly from station to station but I was still too late to attend the presentation. The room was filled to overflowing, no more standing room and the door was closed. I stood in the passageway waiting for the meeting to end. While I was waiting I amused myself looking at books and reading the article in the Tribune about the Book Fair. I heard a loud sound coming from the end of the corridor at uneven intervals. Curiosity got the better of me. I learned it came from the woman's bathroom. Investigating, I found the most amazing hand drier I have ever seen. It sounded like a plane, revving its engines before take off. The power of its wind actually dried hands in just a few minutes. When the door to the meeting room opened, and the crowd thinned I took a seat to wait. Someone asked if I was Beth's mother. We must share a family resemblance, I thought. I regretted not being able to hear fellow classmates, Minerva and Marta read. I regretted it more when I learned that Minerva sang, and I missed it.

Although part of Beth's memoir class, I wasn't part of the day's presentation. I decided to wander the book fair while Beth signed copies of her book. It wasn't long before I regretted that decision. It was hot. Too hot to browse for books and my leg was beginning to suggest I sit down. I found a chair in the sun and listened to the Columbia Jazz Sextet play. Excellent music, but I regretted my place in the sun. Ten minutes and I felt I was well done. Even though I had a chair and could put my feet up, even though I would be able to see Beth and the group coming down the street, even though the music was great, I decided to move. I found a spot standing in the shade by the entrance to Beth's building and met Apollo, a working black Lab and his mistress. We stood listening to the music together. Soon Beth and her party arrived.

Two elevators traveled to the seventh floor, our way guided by one of Beth's sisters. Their apartment at the end of the hall was well suited for a sight challenged person. Once inside, Beth's dog Hanna's attitude changed. At home, free from her collar and harness, she relaxed. The coolness and openness of the apartment allowed everyone to relax.

Entering, you knew music was important to the family. A large black grand piano sat in a corner of the room, sheltering a dog's bed. A big brown bass lay on its side nearby.

The room filled quickly with family and friends. Drinks were provided while Beth's husband Mike and her sisters set out food. A pianist had just returned from his stint as a piano player for a cruise line. The invitation of an open piano was too inviting for him to pass up. Soon music filled the room. The music inspired a singer to accompany him with her beautiful voice. Summertime was one of their selections as others tried to think of songs that they all knew. Soon a songfest began.

Mike's marinated shrimp was a hit. When I learned he was the chef; I asked him to share his recipe and discovered it came from the Pirates House Cookbook, bought while Beth's sister was living in the South. Many of Beth's sisters had the same cookbook but hadn't made the dish.

I complimented Clarice on her beautiful voice and learned she was a vocal coach at St. Francis University in Joliet. One comment led to another and I mentioned I was a practicing Catholic. Soon I found myself telling the story of Pap's passing gift—the day of his wake when a pancake turner dropped out of the carousel in the kitchen. Ten years and a few months have passed since that day and nothing else has fallen out of my carousel.

Clarice suggested I write the story of <u>Pap And The Pancake Turner</u> for Monday's class. I wanted to write about the party.

Minerva's niece serenaded us with her rendition of <u>Nothing Goes Unchanged</u>. Beth and Mike played a duet on piano and bass, a fitting ending to the event

Others went to another author presentation. And I—I went to the Blues Fest.

OUR LADY OF THE UNDERPASS

At Dorothy's surprise 80th birthday party, her son Donnie asked me how I had become so aware. He even suggested that I write a book telling people how to become aware. Then Donnie gave me the perfect opportunity to show him how my life worked. He told me that Our Lady of the Underpass was back. (Even though the image was near my house, I was unaware of the existence until Dorothy told me about the appearance.) I replied that he had just become one of my circle, he was at the right place, at the right time to help me. On the way home from the party, I stopped and took a picture of the new image under the expressway. I gave the picture to Dorothy to share with her son.

By now, you are probably wondering, who is Our Lady of the Underpass? Our Lady of the Underpass was the name given to an image of the Blessed Virgin Mary that appeared under the Chicago expressway in April 2005. Many people gathered at the spot to pray. People waited in long lines to stand before the image. Candles and vases of flowers graced the sidewalk. Pictures of families were placed on the wall. As the crowds grew, both television and the newspapers became involved. Sources stated with authority that it was salt runoff from the highway. The Chicago Catholic Cardinal expressed an opinion. An article in our church bulletin discussed the image. The article said that during a dinner party the subject of Mary's appearance surfaced. A spirited discussion began. A couple of the questions discussed were: why did the image appear on a wall, under the expressway? Why now? "A wise friend answered, 'to get our attention. Look, we are taking time out of our busy lives right now, during this dinner, to talk about faith and God.'"

Someone painted the image black. Someone else tried to restore it. Finally the Department of Streets white washed the wall. Now in 2006, She was back.

After I wrote about Our Lady of the Underpass, I became curious. It is 2007—a year has passed. Was She still there? And I can report that She is. I stopped at the site this summer and saw eighteen candles flickering in the shadows, three vases of fresh roses, a statue of Jesus with two children and a statue of St. Joseph with a child. A picture of Our Lady of Guadalupe has been added. Green vines are filling in the spaces. Plastic flowers in different shades add color. Two garlands, one blue and purple, the other orange and red set the area apart from the rest of the wall. Is it salt run off or an image of Our Lady? Does it matter? Since Her return was not widely advertised, She has been allowed to stay. And it is evident that is important to some people.

In 2006, I took many pictures of the wall. I saw an image above Our Lady. I didn't mention it but I shared the pictures with my family. Both my husband and my daughter Terri saw both images. They mentioned the face to me. They both thought they saw the face of a man. "Don't you see the eyes?" they both asked. I thought it looked like the Son above His Mother but I kept my mouth shut. I had trouble finding the image of Our Lady. Both images are back on the wall.

In 1991, I visited the Queen Of Heaven cemetery in Hillside. The story of that visit is in the early part of this book. Since that time, because of the crowds, the cross has been moved. It has its own spot in the cemetery with its own parking lot. A statue of Our Lady rests on the grass a short distance from the cross. I don't have a special reason for returning to this particular place. I know my prayers are heard wherever I am. But ever so often, I find myself driving to Hillside to visit the cross. Every time I visit, there are always other people there. I often wondered if the unexplained phenomena were continuing or did they stop in 1991. Now our youngest daughter, Sue, has moved to Hillside. We were watching her 16-month son, Daniel, on Friday the week before my husband's second operation for colon cancer. Daniel had just fallen asleep in the car as we approached Sue's house. Rather than cutting his nap short, my husband drove over to the cemetery. He knew it was a quiet place where Daniel would be able to sleep.

I was very surprised to see a woman, sitting in a chair in the shade of a tree, holding a photo album, surrounded by people. I joined the group. I learned that she was not only present in 1991 and had pictures from that time but has many recent photos—a couple showed halos of light resting on top of the cross. She told story after story of unusual phenomena which the photo illustrated. The woman is part of a group that gathers on Sunday afternoon to pray. I was happy to learn that unexplained things still occur.

My daughter Terri visited from Florida after her father's surgery. We stopped at the cross while she was here. Since Daniel was asleep, I remained near the car while she visited the cross. As we drove away, Terri told me that she felt like she was walking in a rose garden. The fragrance of roses was that strong. Since roses in that quantity were not present we know that Our Lady not only visits the place, but She was there.

TA DUM, TA DUM, TA DUM

I was so glad the year 2006 was drawing to a close. It had been a challenging year. I named it THE WATER YEAR. Some good things happened. But most of the year, I felt like the sky was falling. Thankfully, I don't remember everything that happened. Here are the highlights:

The downpour began in February when Terri phoned to tell us she had reached the end of her rope in her marriage and asked Bob for a divorce. He didn't take it well. Tom flew down to Florida to stay with her for a few weeks.

He returned in time to welcome our grandson, Daniel into the world in March—one of the year's bright spots. We told Sue that we were available to help out. Thankfully, she took us up on our offer and we totally enjoyed our new grandson.

We hadn't been able to take a motor home trip in 2005 because of Tom's chemo. We were looking forward to at least one trip in the summer of 2006. In preparation, Good Friday at the camper, we took the blue tarp off the roof of our motor home. Easter Sunday, 6 inches of rain fell. Easter Monday, I opened the motor home to see if we had any rain damage. I noticed some water stains on the bed over the cab. My husband came to help me. When he went into the back bedroom, he saw that our bed was wet. The hatch covering the skylight had blown off. But that wasn't the end of it. When he climbed onto the roof to look at the hinge for the hatch covering, he found two holes in the roof. We phoned the company that worked on our park model trailer. They said they could fix it. I won't bore you with the story. Let's just say that the repair didn't go as planned. We got our motor home back in September, returned it in October and didn't get it back until the Spring of 2007. Any plans for traveling were cancelled.

Drip .. drip .. drip.

On a rainy day, I drove my car to the store. I noticed a stream of gas on the wet street were I had parked. A trip to the mechanic followed. The gas line on my car needed replaced.

Bill phoned. He and his wife had separated; they were trying to work out their marriage problems. After a trial separation, they decided to end their marriage, but remain friends. We told him that he was welcome to move back to our house after they sold theirs.

Brittany, our granddaughter, graduated from high school. Sue, Daniel and I flew to Florida for the ceremony. Benjamin, our first grandson, met his little cousin when he spent the weekend with us. The weather was in the 90's. Soon after we returned, on Memorial weekend, another ulcer surfaced on my leg. I knew from experience that I wouldn't be able to go swimming for another summer.

Sue and her husband, Ivan, finally sold their condo, which was a 10-minute drive from our house. They bought a house in Hillside, close to Loyola Hospital were Doctor Ivan was completing his three-year residency program. Depending on the route we took, they were now 45 minutes away.

Drip .. drip .. drip.

When we bought an unsewered lot at the campground, we didn't even own a tent. After many years, and newer trailers, we had a sewer installed that required a lift station since our lot was on a hill. During the summer, the area around the lift station was wet, even though we didn't have any rain. Investigation showed we had a problem with the lift station that took more than a month to have fixed.

We agreed to watch Daniel three days a week when Sue returned to her teaching job. We decided to rendezvous at her school, a 30-minute drive from our house, for pick up and drop off. Daniel's other grandmother would watch him on Monday and Tuesday.

The ulcer on my leg finally healed in November, a week before Thanksgiving. Now I could go swimming in the pool, except now the pool was closed for the season.

I was so glad to see 2006 end.

New Years day, we were in Chattanooga, TN, preparing to celebrate the marriage of our daughter Terri to Emmett. I was looking forward to 2007. Finally the ulcer on my leg had healed, I was looking forward to a soak in a hot tub or a swim in the pool. The pool wasn't in our building. The temperature outside was too cool to walk outside in a wet bathing suit. I had a nice long shower instead. And it was. When I exited the tub, I discovered a lake on the floor. The shower curtain was outside the tub. Water was everywhere. As I wiped up the water, I hoped I was wiping up the old year.

My first reading of the New Year did not provide comfort. "The rivers will turn foul, the brooks of defense will be emptied and dried up, the reeds and rushes will wither." Isaiah 19:6

I shared the story of my shower with my family, my thought of washing away the old year. I didn't share my reading. The wedding was beautiful. Our trip was delightful. Then we returned home.

I noticed a stream of brown stuff in our upstairs hallway. It seemed to be coming from the wall that housed our chimney. I phoned the man who worked on our chimney. They made repairs.

A couple of weeks passed. Another brown stream in the hallway. Another phone call—a different repair.

Bill's house finally sold. He moved back to our house along with his two pugs, Tidbit and Lexy. Tidbit thought she was the leader of the group. Mabel, our chocolate lab didn't object.

Snow, snowmelt, rain … no stream of brown in the hallway, we thought the problem was fixed. Then it returned. Another phone call. A different solution to the problem—with a cap for the chimney. So far, so good.

March—our grandson's first birthday, a beautiful day that was very warm for March. I hadn't been as careful with sodium since it was winter, my foot swelled. An ulcer surfaced the next week. A friend told me that it was the stress in my life coming out. No swimming again!

We went out to the camper and opened our trailer. As we left for home, I tried to turn off the water into the trailer. It didn't shut off. Another WATER YEAR.

I was worried. I thought I smelled gas in our kitchen. The nightly news told stories about gas explosions destroying homes. I didn't want that to happen to ours. I asked my husband to check the connections on our gas stove. He found nothing. I still smelled gas. I asked if he pulled the stove out and checked the stoves connection at the wall. He explained that he checked the burners. Pulling out the stove didn't reveal a leak either. I still smelled gas. I finally phoned a repairman for service on our stove. Then I turned off the gas connection to our stove in the basement. I was glad that I did. The technician discovered the control in the oven wasn't closing completely, allowing a little bit of gas to escape. He didn't have a repair part in his truck; he would have to order it. We would be without our kitchen stove for a week. Microwave, crock-pot and grill would have to fill in. Then of course, there is always take out.

Pestered to write, I phoned I-Universe to update my publishing notes. Since I had published with them before, I was given a very nice offer if I agreed to publish within a year. Their offer made self-publishing more affordable; my plans that were floating in the air became concrete when I accepted.

We picked up our motor home. It had another leak by the cab but we found a better repairman. Not only did he fix the leak in our motor home, and our water valve going into the trailer, he coated our roof, paying special attention to some cracks. The area was hit by severe rain again but our trailer and our motor home stayed dry.

I had tried for over a year to lose weight. Instead I gained 10 pounds. My diet hadn't changed but the weight wasn't leaving. The extra weight rested on my legs, cutting off the circulation. Tom and I drove to Wisconsin in May to spend a weekend with some friends. The three-hour trip alerted me to the problems I was facing. My legs hurt. We planned to drive to West Virginia in June. The trip would be much longer than three hours. I was worried; I had to do something new.

I made a chart. I numbered the lines from one to thirty-one. At the top of the chart, I listed the various exercises I did. Each day, I checked off what I accomplished. Instead of doing sit ups once a day, I repeated them for a second or third time. When I went too many days without action, I increased my effort. I had my own nag. I managed to lose five pounds. More important, I managed to lose some of my tummy.

Tom is from Maryland. Since most of his family still lived in the surrounding states, he doesn't get the opportunity to visit them. One of his sisters planned a reunion in West Virginia. For health reasons, neither of Tom's brothers nor three of his sisters were able to attend. I felt it was important that we did. Sue and Daniel went back with us. More than 42 family members gathered at the ranch for good company, good food, many laughs and lots of stories. Daniel charmed everyone.

We drove up to Tom's birthplace on the way home. The temperature was in the 90's. I was surprised at the humidity in the mountains. Opening the door of our air-conditioned car, the heat and humidity took my breath away. I thought it would be cooler. Cumberland had changed so much, Tom didn't recognize it. Main streets had been blocked off, creating malls in the downtown area. We had to ask for directions to get out of town.

The day we returned, a hundred-year rain hit our neighborhood. As we drove home, we heard on the radio that the north side of Chicago was hit by heavy rain—many streets were closed, viaducts were flooded, stoplights were out. After we dropped Sue at her house, she phoned her brother to tell him we were on our way. She asked if we had water in the basement. When he went down to check, he found the water, a couple of inches deep, over a large area of our basement. It spread further than it had in years passed, all the way into Tom's workshop. Bill had most of the water vacuumed up before we reached home. We were lucky. It didn't get too deep. I knew that sometimes we got water when the sewers were overloaded so everything touching the floor was waterproof. The next day, talking to neighbors, I learned that water had covered our side street from curb to curb. The water was as high as the doors of some cars. My 1987 Dodge was parked on the side street. Water had seeped in through the rusted holes, soaking the floorboard. A few days of sunshine and open windows dried it out.

My husband's doctor scheduled a colonoscopy. I wasn't worried. I thought everything would be fine. I was wrong. A 3-inch mass had grown in his colon. It had to come out.

Were there messages that something was wrong? Had I missed them? Was I too stressed to notice? Good questions! No answers.

Tests .. surgery .. recovery .. swallowed July and August.

We had hoped to postpone surgery until after we made a road trip. His surgeon didn't think that was advisable. The week before surgery, we watched Daniel, just starting to walk, at his house. My husband was in the bathroom, on the throne. Daniel's bedroom door, his parent's bedroom door and the bathroom door were all closed. Daniel opened all the doors until he found his favorite person, his Pap Pap. When he found him, he wanted up. Thank God for grandchildren! They give us a smile and a laugh.

The week before his surgery, one of Tom's sisters passed. She had Alzheimer's disease and was doing poorly. Then we learned that his brother's wife passed. She had Parkinson's for many years and was also failing. Both were on hospice, both deaths were expected. I told my husband that even though it seemed his family was having a party in heaven, he wasn't supposed to join them. Kathy, our oldest daughter, told me not to worry. The two deaths were expected and except for the mass in his colon, her dad was in good health.

The Sunday before his surgery, we met Kathy and her husband, Mike, at the Renaissance Fair. It was a beautiful day, a welcome change—a step back in time. Sir Walter Raleigh made my day. Walking down the lane, he said, "There she is, me lady." We looked around to see who he was talking to. It was ME! Not only did he bow and kiss my hand, he gave me a white rose. The rose lasted through the day without water, survived the trip home and opened in the vase of water I put it in. Its beauty lasted until my husband was transferred from intensive care to a regular floor in the hospital.

Tom's surgery was successful. The doctor planned to remove Tom's entire colon but decided against it when removal would have jeopardized his kidney. There were no complications but Tom had to spend many days in intensive care because of the various tubes and machines hooked up to his body. He was very happy when he was released a week and a day after his surgery.

Sue and Daniel flew to Florida to visit Terri the day after his surgery. The trip had been planned and airline tickets purchased before we knew there was a mass in Tom's colon. When they returned, Terri and Ben came with them.

Since Terri and Ben were in town, we planned a trip to the Shedd Aquarium. Tom had only been out of the hospital for a few days, so we took advantage of the availability of wheelchairs at the Shedd. Daniel enjoyed riding with his grandfather instead of in his stroller. Since presidential debates where held at Soldier's Field that evening, we had remove our car from the underground garage by 4:00 PM. It is a good thing that Tom decided to go with me to get the car. He thought the walk wouldn't tire him. I couldn't start the car. NOTHING happened. We replaced the car's battery the month before, what could be wrong? The garage was deserted. I would have been in big trouble. Tom checked the battery cables and the car started. We drove the car to our mechanic. He tried to start the car—nothing. The inside of the battery cables were corroded, not making proper contact. Problem solved.

Next the left burner on our automatic ignition gas stove wouldn't light. We tried everything we could think of to fix it. Sometimes it lit; sometimes we had had to use a match.

That same week, a service man came to clean our furnace and discovered that our chimney was blocked. He cleaned out the debris before he left. I decided to call the man who worked on our chimney. I wanted to know if we still had a problem. Sad to say, he failed to show up when expected. He was delayed by a bigger job then fell ill. The question remained, was our chimney safe or did we have a problem?

Daniel was playing with the keyboard and mouse to our computer. Somehow he locked both the keyboard and mouse. Nothing worked. We tried turning the computer off, and rebooting. Still didn't work. Bill is computer savvy. When he came home from work, I presented him with our problem. After he operated— the computer worked.

As if that wasn't enough things going wrong, I lost a bunch of blank checks. I didn't carry my checkbook with me but I carried the check pad. I reached for a check at a store and couldn't find one. I looked everywhere. I searched the house. I called or stopped in at the places I had visited without success. Luckily, I don't have our full name on the checks, only our first initial. I debated calling the bank to block the checks but at $15 or is it $30 per check, it was a substantial bit of money. I called the banks teller phone everyday for over a week, hoping that none of the checks would show up. They didn't.

Every time we asked a doctor if my husband could go to the country, we received a negative answer. Tom was NOT pleased. Finally he received the green light. Two days before we planned to leave, another storm hit the north side of Chicago. Over 300 trees were uprooted and branches were down everywhere, blown down by strong winds. Thousands of homes were without electric—for days. Our block must have been under a dome because I didn't see any damage. Listening to the news on television, many of the reports of downed trees came from areas around our house. When I ventured out, the area looked like a war zone. Luckily, this time we didn't get water in our basement. I phoned friends at the campground to see if we would be able to reach our trailer. In heavy rains, a few roads were closed. I was relieved when I learned that all roads were open.

The lab reports were encouraging, no cancer in the liver or lymph nodes. The surgeon removed all the damaged tissue plus a safe margin but chemo was strongly recommended to destroy any remaining cancer cells. I called it weed control. His oncologist didn't think we should take a road trip before starting chemo. We listened. Tom started treatments again on 9/11. A series of twelve is planned which will continue, every other week, for at least 6 months.

NUDGED

The month of September was rapidly passing. I knew I needed to write but I had neither the time nor the energy nor the words. School was back in session, we watched Daniel three days a week, I had less free time. If I wanted to have the book finished this year, I had to get busy.

The second weekend of September, I attended a woman's retreat with Sue, my youngest daughter. In a skit, one of the actresses prayed, "Lord, give me the words." I could easily relate with the feeling. I felt BLOCKED.

Fall was arriving on Sunday, another weekend was here and I had not even turned on my computer. I decided to start putting the stories into book form. I started with the first three: Introduction, In The Beginning and Tracking Time. Since I didn't know what I was doing, I decided to get a hard copy of my efforts. I had successfully linked the three pieces. But I lost the formatting, the indentation on the paragraphs and the print changed on three paragraphs of In The Beginning.

I was reminded of the "Help" I received when I was working on *To Pap With Love,* the print changed on that book too. Monday morning I phoned the assistant who was assigned to help me bring the book to life. I learned she was no longer with the company. I was assigned a new assistant; she didn't have the answer to my predicament but she did offer to look over my mess before I submitted it as a book.

So my week began, a week I'm referring to as self-destruct. After my phone discussion, I left in my car, an old 1987, dented, rusting Dodge Shadow, which always started … every time, even in the coldest weather and ran without problems. Until Monday! Kathy, my oldest daughter, was undergoing tests at Loyola Hospital, than planning to visit Brookfield zoo. I decided to join her. I saw bumper-to-bumper traffic on the Kennedy expressway so I changed my plans, driving through the parks instead until I reached the Eisenhower expressway. I was happy with my decision; it was an uneventful ride until I got on the expressway. Normally my car reached 50 or 60 miles per hour in a minute or two. I had my foot all the way down to the floorboard and I was only going 45. I got a sick feeling in my stomach. Something was wrong. I held my foot to the floor, the car went into overdrive, I reached the speed of 50 for a minute or two, then the speed decreased to 45. By the time I reached my exit, I had decided to turn around and go home. I didn't know if I should take the streets or the expressway. Which would be safer? I pulled over to a side street and phoned my husband to alert him to my problems. I left a message for Kathy, telling her my plans had been changed. I decided to take the expressway. All the way back I encouraged my car, telling it I knew it could get me home. For a couple of minutes, I thought my problems had ended but it was a false hope. I decided not to drive into the loop, but took the parkway system back to the north side. A car stopped quickly in front of me in the middle of the park, but I had no problems stopping. When I drove into our mechanic's garage, I pulled to the side and turned off my car. Then I explained the problems I had with my car.

I wasn't home very long before I received a phone call from our mechanic. He knew my car's problem. He said the front brakes on my car were locked and had been locked for a long time. The brake cylinders were red hot. He couldn't move my car.

His remark explained the heat I felt in the car as I reached the garage. I looked at the gauges and the temperature was normal, the heater was off. I hadn't mentioned that the car felt hot to the mechanic, thinking it was my imagination or a hot flash.

On the way to the garage I had thought about the age of my car. Should we have it repaired? I knew we couldn't afford to replace my car. With watching our grandson three days a week and Tom's chemo treatments, I didn't feel we could only have one car. We didn't seem to have a choice. We needed to fix my car.

Monday night, I wanted popcorn. Our son's two pugs and Mabel, our chocolate Lab enjoyed popcorn too. I planned to make enough for the four of us. Except the top of the popcorn maker came apart, dumping popcorn kernels all over the floor. With the help of a broom, I got most of the kernels up. Starting over, it almost happened again. This time I was able to stop the kernels from falling all over the floor. Not deterred, I made a batch of popcorn. As I was sharing the popcorn with the dogs, I felt like I had a stone in my mouth. It wasn't a stone but a part of my tooth. I hadn't bit down on anything hard that would have caused the tooth to break. It had been years since I visited a dentist; I always had a leg ulcer. I was waiting for the ulcer on my leg to heal before making the call. The popcorn changed my plans.

Tuesday was uneventful. I spent the day with a friend. When I got home I phoned the dentist's office. I told the receptionist that I broke a tooth but it wasn't an emergency. I was able to make an appointment for Friday. That evening I worked on a Christmas present for Sue.

Wednesday morning before the sun was up, I walked over to our upstairs bathroom in the dark. I saw Mabel lying on the floor by the stairs. Leaving the bathroom, blinded by the light, I forgot Mabel was lying by the stairs. I tripped over her, but used my hands to block my fall. She was unhurt but I damaged my right wrist.

Wednesday night, the Northshore storytelling guild was holding their monthly meeting in a new location. I hadn't attended a guild meeting in a couple of years; they met in a northern suburb, more difficult for me to drive home from at night when I was tired. At a Folk concert in July, I met a storytelling friend and learned they had a new meeting place, close to my home. I asked her to let me know the date of the next meeting. Since I had a damaged right wrist, which would prevent my writing or working on my daughter's Christmas present, I decided to go to the meeting

The guild was meeting at a Nature Center in the heart of the city, a short drive from my house. Arriving early, I met four deer, enjoying their evening snack at dusk. It was a welcome greeting. The place was so quiet I wondered if I was at the right place when more people arrived. It was nice to hear stories again. I didn't have a story prepared. When pressed, I told the story of my self-destruct week. A regular storyteller remarked that he remembered I always told spiritual stories.

Friday, I went to Mass to say thank you for helping me to survive the week. I often became the lecturer for the first reading and the psalm response on Friday. I find there is a difference when I hear someone else read the words or when I proclaim them. Friday was the feast day of St. Matthew, one of the apostles chosen by Jesus. I read: "It was he who gave some to be apostles, some to be prophets, some to be evangelists, and some to be pastors and teachers." Ephesians 4:11 The response from Psalm 19: "Their message goes out through all the earth." In his homily Fr. Steve told us, "We are called to discipleship. Our faith isn't meant to be put under a bushel basket but shared with others."

Although we planned to go to the country for the weekend, my appointment with the dentist delayed our leaving until Saturday. I was able to attend A Taste Of The Holy Land, the dinner for volunteers held Friday night at our church. A gentleman complimented me on my reading of the scriptures and suggested I teach the readers on Sunday how to use the mike. Someone else said they always recognized my voice even when they couldn't see me. Another friend told me I had a distinctive walk, she could always recognize me walking down the street. I remembered how recently a voice from a car called as I walked down the street, "Someone is always watching you." And I had laughed. As part of the decorations, golden coins were spread on the table. I ignored them until a friend gave me one. "Here, this is for you," Marsha told me. As I looked at the coin, I saw the words: "I can do all things through Christ who strengthens me Philippians 4:13."

NUDGED, AGAIN!

THE JOURNEY
CONTINUES

Do you ever feel like the sky is falling? Do you ever feel like you shouldn't have gotten out of bed? Or do you feel that you should go back to bed and stay there? That feeling doesn't change when you become more aware.

I use a weekly engagement calendar to try to keep track of my life. Not that all kinds of interesting things happen, quite the contrary. The events of today will have pushed the events of last week completely out of my mind. Since the engagement calendar that I use has beautiful photos and inspirational words, I open it at random every day. I jot down the day's date on the page.

I began writing Ta Dum, Ta Dum on September 23. This morning, October 1, I opened my engagement calendar to the week of August 6. On the right hand margin, the title Ta Dum stared back at me on the page. I was reminded of the challenging things that happened that week, challenges that I had not included. The first week of August, I was extremely busy, but writing was not on my to-do list. Tom had just gotten out of the hospital. Terri and Ben, daughter and first grandson, were visiting from Florida.

Life doesn't become easier as you become more aware.

Will reading my journey help you? Are the obstacles rising one after another in my life meant to stop this journey from coming to print? Or are they there to make me more determined, to reinforce my resolve to finish this book? Interesting questions—no answers.

I have been happily surprised by some of the things I have discovered putting this book together. Events that were written fresh, when they happened are alive, full of details that I have forgotten.

Sad to say, my notes are not complete. I jotted down the major details, omitting the fine points, thinking I would remember. I DON'T!

I didn't immediately recognize all the help I received. It was a gradual process. I didn't write down all the times I was hit on the head: twig, branch, broom, food from the refrigerator, or freezer, stuff off the shelves—at home, and in a store, the trunk cover of my car. Sometimes my head hurt; sometimes I was puzzled—wondering what I was supposed to do. Sometimes I had to laugh—shopping at Wal-Mart, a diet aid fell into my cart. This year I realized that events that seem perfectly normal to me would have astounded me in the past and I realized how far I've come. My father has been gone for over 12 years. He still "helps" me, but he is not the only one. I no longer give credit to one person for the "help" I receive, I just say thank you!

The ulcer on my leg still hasn't healed. It hasn't gotten bigger or deeper, maintaining its status quo. Why did it stop healing? Stress or life or less exercise? Another good question!

The chimney man showed up on our doorstep this week. He is supposed to return on Tuesday to make some repairs. He wasn't feeling well. Hmm!

I'm pleased to report that our chimney has now been repaired. One less thing to worry about!

My statement in CATHEDRAL surprised me when I read the comment to the line: "Be Not Afraid, I go before you. Come follow me and I will give you peace." My comment was: "These words give me confidence to walk through the day and not worry about tomorrow." At the time, I thought *To Pap, With Love* would be published and would sell many copies. I thought the book would make a positive difference in my life. It did, but not in the way I expected. From the feedback I have received from the people who have read it, it helped them with their lives.

I will admit that I no longer devote the time to worrying that I used to. I was a champion at making a molehill into Mount Everest in a heartbeat. Without warning I found myself on the edge of the cliff, panicked. Since I know I can't walk on water, I bundle my problems and give it to the One who can. Do I still worry? Sometimes. It is easier to remain worry free when the road is smooth, the water calm. It is harder when bumps and boulders obstruct the road, when storms come and the waves engulf me. Sometimes my body worries for me. Do I still plan? Does God still laugh?

In the evening, after I wrote the above paragraph, Sue phoned concerned about Daniel. He has been sick for too many days, she was taking him to the doctor the next day. Immediately I found myself swimming to keep afloat as huge waves threatened to drown me. Then I started my wireless calls to God—all evening, all night, whenever I woke, I called. After all, God never sleeps! Even though Daniel wasn't much better the next night, the doctors weren't worried. And neither was I.

I realized that my family is what pushes my worry button. I don't necessarily worry about myself or money or things. I wish I could say that I immediately put my worries in God's hands. Sometimes I do, sometimes I scale a mountain or sink to the bottom of the lake before making the call.

Once again, it is Fall Festival at the campground, a fitting time to end this story. I attended the surprise birthday party of a 70-year-old friend. During the party an acquaintance asked how she knew me. I mentioned three or four or five places we could have met. And she responded, "You're all over the place, just like a horse fly". And I was reminded of the time that Rosie, a close friend, called me a fart on the wind. I guess I still am.

Once again Fall Festival was special. I woke from a dream in which I understood why Tom had to undergo chemo again as well as a not so gentle nudge to lose weight. Even though it was 4:00 AM, I was not allowed to go back to sleep. I even promised not to forget the message of my dream. It made no difference. I finally got up and began my morning ritual. I randomly opened the bible to Daniel 4:8. "Finally, Daniel came into my presence and I told him the dream". Message received. Notes made. I was allowed to go back to sleep.

We went to 4:15 Mass on Saturday afternoon. I opened to the song God Who Stretched the Spangled Heavens, and read, "May it challenge us anew.... Children of creative purpose, Serving others, honoring you."

My notebook was home on the dining room table. I jotted a couple of notes on the church bulletin. Father's homily frosted the cake: "Trust God's plan" and "Use the talents he gave us."

The flea market had a couple of toys for Daniel that were made before recalls of toys made in China became a major worry for parents of young children. Sing with me, "Christmas is coming, the goose is getting fat...."

We took Daniel to his first pumpkin hunt. He liked ALL the pumpkins.

I told the story of Tracking Time at our morning coffee get together. This evening a friend who was at the morning coffee told me a of a chance meeting she had with a complete stranger where she shared her life experience to help him with his own problem. I asked her to think about their chance meeting and all the other times she has been at the right place, at the right time to help someone. I was reminded of another of the reasons for sharing my stories—"to help others see."

I love the line from Robert Frost's poem <u>The Road Not Taken</u>. "Two roads diverged in a wood, And I,—I took the one less traveled by, And that has made all the difference."

978-0-595-45152-4
0-595-45152-7

www.ingramcontent.com/pod-product-compliance
Lightning Source LLC
Chambersburg PA
CBHW051249050326
40689CB00007B/1119